Where There's Hope

All best wishes!

Hope Mihalap

WHERE THERE'S HOPE

There's Life and Laughter

Hope Mihalap

Trudy Knox, Publisher
Granville, Ohio

WHERE THERE'S HOPE

Trudy Knox, Publisher
168 Wildwood Drive
Granville, OH 43023-1073

Judith A. Johnson, Editor
Newark, OH

Cover Photograph
Chip Gamertsfelder

First Edition
ISBN: 0-9611354-6-8
LCN: 93-081185

CONTENTS

FOREWORD

The first time I saw Hope Mihalap on a stage I knew I was watching a speaker who not only marched to a different drummer, she brought an entire orchestra in her head to share with the world in the most unique way I have ever experienced. It was like the reincarnation of Gilda Radner combined with a touch of Bea Lillie, Elayne Boosler and Martha Raye in her heyday.

She made me laugh as few people ever had. My guess was that she had lived a fascinating life full of characters that she observed and then had the genius to give life to on the platform. This book has proven my guess to be on target.

When Hope asked me to write the Foreword to her book, I read it to get a feel for it, of course. But I did not anticipate copying entire chapters to send to our kids, or insisting that my husband shut off the TV while I read just one more hilarious story to him. I laughed aloud and every so often reflected on her innate wisdom. I rejoice in being able to call her my friend.

You will want to share this book with those you love. It is one of those rare, honest reflections that will bring back reminiscences of another time and another place. And despite the fact that our ethnic backgrounds are different from hers we realize that although we come from different roots, we were planted in common soil.

That is a lot for a humorist to accomplish in a book. But, oh, until you have had your facial muscles hurt from laughing so much or had your streaking mascara make you look like a raccoon from watching her on a stage with her accents, dialects, outrageous theatrics, all woven into stories that will leave you in awe of her intelligence and insight, "you ain't seen nothin' yet!"

She is one of the few SILLY women I know. I giggle with abandon around her. You will, too. From opera to child-rearing, her reflections will cause you to know that where there's Hope, there's laughter—and much, much more. Enjoy! Just be forewarned. Your funny bone is in for more exercise than you have given it in a long time.

ROSITA PEREZ, Speaker and Author
President, Creative Living Programs, Inc.

I

FROM SCHLITZ TO ICONS

When I was two years old, Uncle Kallimachos stood me up on the kitchen table and taught me to spell Budweiser, Schlitz and Pabst. An audience consisting of my parents, two aunts, three uncles, my grandmother and a great-aunt clapped, cheered and shouted bravos. This led me into show business.

Well, you really can't call it show business. That implies film, television, stage, touring, celebrity, drink, drugs, tranquilizers and divorce. My life is milder than this. It is possible to make a living—on a less exalted scale—simply by holding a microphone and telling humiliating stories about yourself and your family. If the stories are long and you ridicule principally yourself, you're a humorist. If you condense the material to one-liners and talk about sex, politics, or celebrities, you're a comedienne. If you go out of town to talk, you make more money than if you stay where people know you.

The basic requirement in being a humorist is finding enough peculiar events in your life story to share with the public. The fact that Uncle Kallimachos really did have that name and taught me the things he did gave me a fine head start.

I'm a Greek from Norfolk, Virginia, which already has interesting possibilities. As the only child of Penny and Chris Christopoulos, I was lucky enough to be surrounded by Greek-Americans with alert senses of the ridiculous. This is not typical, let me assure you.

There is generally a sort of moroseness or Mediterranean angst among Greek-Americans. Many of the men own restaurants, and this leads to Olympian worry over lack of customers, drunken cooks and relatives-you-employ-who-turn-out-to-be-racketeers. The women among the earliest immigrant families were powerful mother-figures who terrorized misbehaving children by whacking them with long wooden spoons and flying bedroom slippers. In most cases, these trembling children grew up to be successful businessmen and women who appeared to adore their tyrannical mothers.

At the Greek Orthodox church, where all Greek-Americans meet, the nationality's natural affinity for politics manifests itself in parish council debates, angry factions, disputes with the priest and fierce jockeying for political posts. Rarely do Greek-Americans carry these talents over into a non-Greek community area, such as a civic club. They prefer to argue with their fellow Greeks.

My maternal grandfather, George Christopoulos—same last name as my paternal grandfather—was so unlike his wife that you wonder how they ever became attracted to each other in the first place and how, even more miraculously, they stayed together for life. Family anecdotes tell us they met in the little village of Silimna in Tripoli, a region of the Greek Peloponnese. Papou—all Greek grandfathers are called Papou—was, I am told, terrifically handsome and dashing and was considered a little wild. Yaya—the Greek word for all grandmothers—was spunky, strong-willed and cute. Her name was Paraskevi Papoulias.

Yaya's father was a successful wine merchant and innkeeper. Yaya knew that some day her parents would arrange a marriage for her and she would head her own domestic realm, so she laid plans early on to be the best cook and matriarch that the village could possibly produce. There was a fierce spirit of competition among the village girls in these respects.

Accordingly, Yaya would sneak into the big kitchen of the inn whenever traveling dignitaries stopped there during their tedious journeys through the mountains. Influential Athenians often took their French cooks along with them on trips to alleviate the hardships of rough accommodations. Yaya would hide behind a cabinet or stove to watch the foreign cooks prepare unusual dishes, storing the information in her sharp young mind so that she might prepare staggeringly original dishes later as a wife, thereby confounding the other village girls who knew only ordinary local cuisine.

This is why Yaya, as a young mother later in Virginia, would surround a crown roast of pork with honey-glazed onions or serve braised rabbit with garlic-walnut sauce or chicken livers with green onions and fennel. It was hard to find another Greek woman who could match the originality of her dishes.

Papou, riding majestically about the village on horseback, black eyes sparkling and moustache bristling, noticed the confident young woman and wanted her for a wife. Her family was ill at ease because this young man was known to be ambitious and a little hot-tempered, but they acquiesced. The young couple was married on July 26, 1898. The wedding invitation, which according to village tradition was sent out not by the bride's parents but by the bridegroom, is on fading but elegant parchment paper and sits framed in a curio cabinet in my living room.

Within three years their lives changed drastically. Two unconnected but equally shocking events brought about their decision to come to the United States. The first, an unspeakable tragedy, was the deaths of their first two children on the same day. An infant son succumbed to pneumonia; their toddler daughter was scalded to death, having fallen into one of the great cauldrons of boiling water being used to humidify the infant's sickroom.

Yaya, nearly insane with grief, was on the verge of a breakdown. Not long after the tragedy, Papou went to the town hall to cast his vote in a national election. Following the voting custom of his region, he dropped a black ball, the symbol of a negative vote, into the box of the royalist candidate. Two unprincipled election officials spotted the gesture and challenged his choice. In the ensuing dispute, Papou cut off the ear of one of the officials and was arrested and put in jail.

In the middle of the night, Yaya's father helped his son-in-law escape from jail, gave the young couple his blessing and whatever goods he could spare and sent them by horse and buggy in the darkness to the port of Patras. They went first to Italy; six months later, they were able to arrange passage to America.

Unfortunately I never met my grandfather, but my mother described him in a voice rich with love and longing, for he was her favorite person in the world and she grew up to be exactly like him. For all the accounts of his hot-tempered behavior in Greece, he was also a dreamer, incredibly prescient in real estate, an admirer of beautiful things, a businessman with the soul of a poet. His wife had no patience with him, brushing him off when he would approach her in the kitchen to hand her a bouquet of violets as she prepared dinner.

Papou did extremely well from the beginning after he settled in Norfolk, Virginia. He chose Norfolk for an odd reason. Relatives had already immigrated to Ohio and Papou and Yaya went there first. But they encountered an Ohio winter and didn't like it. Papou took out a map of the world and laid a ruler straight across from his Greek village to the area on America's east coast that seemed closest in latitude. It turned out to be Norfolk. Had he wished for similarity in climate, he would have done better to go to California, but he was unaware of the strange disparities in coastal weather, regardless of latitudes.

They liked Norfolk. Within a short time, Papou opened first one and then a chain of shoe-shine parlors. These had red plush carpets, crystal chandeliers and beautiful shoe-shine chairs of polished mahogany. The shoe-shine boys were youngsters from Tripoli, Greece, whom Papou sponsored for immigration. Each week he put their wages into individual savings accounts, allowing them to keep their tips. When the boys reached age eighteen or $1000 in savings, they were offered the choice of staying on with Papou in one of his business enterprises, which by then included the opening of the first movie theater in Norfolk, or going to Chicago where another Tripoli native was prepared to give them work. Most chose Chicago.

Papou, Yaya and their six children had a big house in Norfolk and a summer house on a little lake next to Chesapeake Bay. One afternoon Papou took my mother out

Circa 1919
Top row, left to right: My mother (Penelope), Aunt Connie, Yaya, Aunt Helen. Bottom row, left to right: Uncle Kelly, Papou, Uncle Chris, Uncle Teddy.

into the yard of the summer house and pointed over to the expanse of the bay. "Someday, little doe," he told her in Greek, "there will be a big road going right across that water all the way to New York." My mother ran home to report this wondrous news to her mother. Yaya, slapping pots around the kitchen, snapped at her husband, "George, what's the matter with you? Are you crazy? How can there be a road across the water? Stop telling the children these foolish dreams."

In the 1950's, preparations began for the construction of the great Chesapeake Bay Bridge-Tunnel, an eighteen-mile engineering marvel that would span the bay. My grandmother, in her eighties, had watched her sons negotiate the sale of the old summer house that stood near the site. The tunnel authority chose to burn the old timbers and shingles of the demolished house rather than go to the trouble of hauling them away. Our family observed this conflagration with pleasure, feeling that the smoke drifting heavenward from the great bonfire might carry with it the spirit of laughter and festivity that had been so much a part of the old place. The first section of the immense bridge-tunnel—which leads straight across the bay to the Eastern Shore of Virginia, connecting directly to the highway to New York—stands over the exact spot where my grandfather stood that afternoon with his favorite child.

When my mother was born, my grandmother refused to hold or nurse her because she was the third girl. Village women of her vintage wanted sons. Papou took the baby in his arms and went over to the icon that hung in the dining room, with the flickering votive lamp before it. He held the infant up to the icon and proclaimed, "God, give me ten more exactly like this one!" Then he carried the baby to his wife and laid it in her arms.

"Feed her, Paraskevi!" he ordered. "This is the one that will close my eyes when I die." Nobody ever told my mother this anecdote during her father's lifetime.

The Depression ruined him financially; he died of heart failure at age fifty-two. When he took his last breath in the little beach house on the Chesapeake Bay, my grandmother did what Greek wives always did: she screamed, ran from the room sobbing dirges and fainted. My mother, sitting quietly by her father's bedside, leaned over and gently closed his eyes.

My father was born in Cyprus, which mainland Greeks consider an affliction of sorts, and came to the United States at the age of nineteen. He was handsome, dashing, well-bred and intellectual. My mother, one of the first Americans of Greek descent to be born in Virginia, had never met a Greek like him before. At thirteen, knowing that her family would never permit her to marry a non-Greek, she set her sights on him at once. They found something to joke about right away. They had the same last name, even though there was absolutely no relationship between their families.

Though my mother was still a girl, the cosmopolitan young Cypriot noticed her right away and kept her in mind, because she was the least spoiled and most unaffected of the three Christopoulos daughters, the most enterprising and certainly the prettiest. He greatly admired the father of the Christopoulos girls, recognizing in him a man of intelligence and quality, and decided that this would be the family he would most like to join through matrimony. They would have married when Mama was in her early twenties except that she was the third daughter, and Greek tradition dictated that the older girls had to marry first. They could have defied this tradition—in movies or novels they would have—but in real life first-generation Greek-Americans obeyed their parents. Besides, my grandmother would have screamed and fainted a lot and my mother wasn't up to coping with her. For six years they were secretly engaged, and Mama would smile at her own sisters' fluttery crushes on young Chris Christopoulos.

Daddy had a sharp wit and was a skilled raconteur. Though I may be prejudiced, I would say he held an audience better than most people I had ever met, especially among the other Greek orators of Norfolk. He was also an excellent debater and presider, using clever, ironic vocabulary to make his points. He should have been a lawyer; this was his family's intention. In fact he had gone for one year to law school in Athens; then when civil war closed down the university in 1919, as a lark he came to America. Like most of the other young men who came

Daddy by his new Auburn, cutting a dashing figure in his courtship days.

over then, he fell prey to the easy money of a small business with a busy cash register and never went back to college.

Years later I asked why he couldn't have gone to law school at night and maybe let my mother work part-time to help pay the bills. "A wife supporting a HUSBAND?" he cried, scandalized.

And so he used his adversarial wit at church meetings and spent all his leisure time reading court stories, biographies, adventures and satires. He joined every available book club and my mother covered all the walls of an extra bedroom with shelves to house the volumes. When they sold their home, they sent all the books to our house and we had to build an extra room to accommodate them, but it was worth it. Every time I look at the titles and worn bindings I picture him in his armchair in the living room, elbow propped on the left arm of the chair, book in his left hand, his right hand reaching over to turn a page or lift a demi-tasse of Turkish coffee to his lips as he devoured the wonderful phrases that he himself might have invented to transfix a jury.

My mother, if born in different times to a less conservative family, could have been a fine architect. Or a great real-estate tycoon. Or a designer, or an artist. If the Depression had not come and her father had not died, she might have been allowed to go to college, provided one of her sisters accompanied her as a chaperone. What she really wanted to do and had asked to do, shocking the family, was to go away to art school. But girls didn't leave home to do Bohemian things.

Mama as she looked when I was eleven years old.

Instead, she took painting lessons and designed and made clothes for herself, her sisters and later for me. She rebuilt and constructed and planned and decorated and painted, inside and out, every house she ever lived in. And she worked from morning until night at hard labor in family businesses after her father died, to help her mother, brothers and sisters survive the Depression. She was good-looking, vivacious, charmingly at ease in every social situation and totally devoid of pretense. No wonder my father fell in love with her.

What always amazed me the most about my mother, though, was how she seemed to know, simply by nature, how to be a good mother. Her role model had been a no-nonsense, old-fashioned Greek matriarch with a battering wooden spoon who made no secret of the fact that she loved her oldest son best. Yaya did not spare the rod nor indulge any sensitivities among her children. Yet they loved her—perhaps because, after all, she had a sense of humor and would kill for her family. And you couldn't quarrel very much with that.

But I preferred the instincts of my own mother, who went against the child-raising fashions of the early thirties by doing such things as breast feeding me until I was two years old, hiding behind doors to do it because the establishment considered it barbaric, holding me when I cried, talking and playing with me, letting me interrupt her gossip with a neighbor when I had some exciting new discovery to show her. People reportedly pursed their lips together in disapproval when she did these things, muttering, "That child's going to run your life some day." Without consulting any New Mother handbooks, she sensed that there was a difference between paying attention and spoiling—a difficult judgment to call but one which she determined unerringly every time.

And though she and my father had both been struck frequently as children, they belied the traditional theory that abuse begets abuse, for they never laid a hand on me—a concept of child-rearing to which my husband and I also subscribe, to the disgust of some next-door neighbors years ago who used to tell us, with nods and glances at each other, "Those children of yours need a good whipping. You better show them who's boss RIGHT NOW, while they're still little." Presumably, it was a good idea to get 'em while they were still defenseless or else you could lose your advantage.

My father's mother, Cypriot Yaya, was the one for whom I was named. Her name, Elpis—fortunately pronounced el-PEACE—means Hope in English. She was eccentric, a polite way of describing someone who drives everybody in the family insane. She was a compulsive buyer and collector, bankrupting her husband Polykarpos, a gentle, aristocratic judge who had once been a professor of English at Robert College in

Istanbul. Their four children were all extremely bright and emotional, subject to great swings of mood, excellent in drama or rhetoric. All these unusual genes produced marvelous cousins, whom we rarely see, unfortunately, because they all live in Cyprus or England.

If Daddy hadn't come to the United States in 1919 and put an ocean between himself and his mother, she would have bankrupted him too. In fact, she almost did; he sent her money on demand every month, even during the Depression, never knowing she didn't really need it but was losing it playing poker.

All along one of our living room walls are Greek and Russian icons. Cypriot Yaya collected them over the years. She also collected ancient pottery, Russian emigre artifacts, Asian porcelain and paintings. These, too, are in our possession—not because we understand them or are collectors but because Cypriot Yaya, as wildly generous as she was extravagant, gave them to my parents when we visited Cyprus in 1946.

She said to my awe-struck mother, "You like these things? You're the only one in the family besides me who does. Take them all to America with you."

We emptied the big steamer trunks we had brought with us to Cyprus full of American consumer goods and refilled them with the antiques and icons. Among the icons is a particularly handsome one of St. George and the Dragon. I know how Yaya got that one. Cypriot families used to take vacations at monasteries—lovely places for vacations even if the rooms were a little spare and there was no indoor plumbing. The food was good, the monks were interesting, the scenery was beautiful. There were vineyards outside the monastery walls where you could pick your own grapes for lunch and cool them in an icy mountain stream.

And after dinner at night, when there wasn't much else to do, visitors could play little games with the monks. Yaya played cutthroat poker. When she lost, she contributed a little something to the monastery's charities. But one night she was the decisive winner. The abbot, a kindly, bearded old man, said, "What kind of winnings could we possibly pay you, Mrs. Christopoulos? We're poor monks."

Yaya said, "That's a nice icon of St. George and the Dragon over there."

Whenever a clergyman visits my house and admires the icons, I like to point out that a couple of them are poker winnings.

When Daddy left Cyprus for America in 1919, he thought he would be gone no more than a year. Business turned out to be fairly good in Norfolk and he had met lovely young Penelope Christopoulos, so he didn't hurry back. Word reached him in the mid-1920's that his father was gravely ill; he started back for a visit. While he was at sea on his way to Cyprus, his father died. His admiration for his father was boundless and he often described him with the same degree of longing and total love that my mother conveyed when describing her late father. From everything they said, I gathered that these two grandfathers whom I had never had the pleasure of meeting were alike in many ways: affectionate, wise and intelligent. In both cases, they had married women of forceful character, dynamos who fascinated them but were as unlike them as night is to day.

Despite his mother's pleas, Daddy came back to the United States, assuming he would return before long for another visit. Months stretched into years, and the Depression preempted any travel plans he might have had in mind. It would be almost twenty years before he saw his relatives again, but he was preoccupied with other things. In 1933 Penny Christopoulos' older sisters finally married, one right after the other. This meant they didn't have to wait any longer: Penny and Chris married on New Year's Eve, 1933.

My mother did the usual things most Depression-era girls did in anticipation of their weddings. She made her own white satin dress and all the bridesmaids' dresses, just as she had designed and made her sisters' bridesmaids' gowns earlier that year.

The gowns sewn for her sister Connie's wedding were, in fact, involved in a harrowing event two days before the ceremony. Everyone was asleep in the old beach house where the family now lived year-round when there was a sudden roaring and then a thunderous crash. It was about six A.M. Everyone jumped out of bed and ran around yelling and bumping into things until someone shouted, "It came from the attic!" My grandmother rushed up the narrow steps to the attic, where all the wedding clothes and presents were being stored. There, protruding halfway through the wall into the house, was the front end of a single-engine airplane. The pilot, alive but dazed, sat slumped in the cockpit, teeth knocked out, blood trickling from a forehead wound.

In the plane's propeller, still slowly rotating, was a shred of green cloth. It was a piece of curtain, but it was the same color as a bridesmaid's dress. Yaya rushed over to the cockpit, shook her fist in the face of the wounded pilot and yelled, "You sonofabeech; you ruined my daughter's wedding!" "I'm sorry, ma'am," he gasped, his eyes rolling backward. We still have the AP photo of the rear end of the plane sticking out of the attic.

The pilot who dropped by, May, 1933.

As for Mama's wedding, she made it as glamorous as possible under stringent financial circumstances. There were no resources for glamorous parties and presents and clothes, and she longed for at least one touch of elegance to dignify the newspaper account for the Norfolk society page. They finally hit on something: Daddy's late father in Cyprus had been a judge. Mama submitted the following information to the paper in her wedding announcement: "Mr. Christopoulos is the son of the late Judge Christopoulos of Cyprus." The newspaper printed it "Mr. Christopoulos is the son of the late Jud Christopoulos of Cypress, Va."

Everybody in the family got married in the dining room of the beach house. An hour before my parents' wedding, Great-Aunt Skookie went up into the attic to look for a hat she wanted to wear, stepped off the wooden flooring onto an unstable area and fell partway through the dining room ceiling. Her left leg was suspended in its entirety over the altar, where little drifts of plaster wafted winningly over the bridal wreaths and candles. They yanked her up about ten minutes before the priest arrived.

2

HOLY KNOCKS AND PICNICS

When I was born my parents were living in a tiny apartment in downtown Norfolk, but all major festive events continued to take place in the beach house. My christening occurred in that same fateful dining room, with a great bronze font borrowed from the Greek church, which was being painted. The font was set up right under the chandelier and when the priest picked me up and intoned, "In the name of the Father . . . ," he banged my head on the chandelier. No doubt this holy knock on the head shaped my peculiar outlook on life for decades to come.

Being an only child, only niece and only grandchild on my mother's side of the family, I was also the exciting new plaything of the clan. This had positive results. Uncle Kelly—the Kallimachos of whom you read before—had never married or had children of his own, so he enjoyed turning other people's offspring into entertaining projects.

Every time we went to my grandmother's house my uncles and aunts, all of whom lived with Yaya, surrounded me and taught me things. The beer names were one of the tamest lessons. Flushed with his success at having me spell the brands correctly at age two-and-a-half, Uncle Kelly moved on to more exotic vocabulary. Soon I could say "pimp," "manure," and "butt" in Greek. These were crowd-pleasers as long as I was small. The moment it appeared that I knew what the words meant, they ceased to amuse the audience.

Uncle Kelly also taught me to read when I was about three. Newspaper headlines came first, then billboards and signs. Once I really caught on I began to read a few things for pleasure before starting school. This is why the Dick and Jane primers in first grade puzzled me. I couldn't figure out why they wasted so much space on each page with those huge drawings of Dick, Jane and Spot, leaving only a little room at the bottom for one or two words such as "Run, Spot, run."

This dainty flower girl had an extensive and unusual Greek vocabulary.

"This is dumb," I said to the little boy who sat next to me. "Why don't they write more words on the page?" He stared at me and put his finger in his nose.

The teacher said, "Hope, stop talking." This was a phrase I was to hear intermittently about 50 percent of the time in elementary school. It's a good thing I ignored it or I would never have gotten into performing.

The uncles and my parents also supplied me with pencils and paper, because they saw that I had a predilection for cartooning, just as our own daughter Tamara does now. I might even have considered a career in art if it hadn't been for Mrs. Snyder in kindergarten.

Mrs. Snyder was built like the Queen Elizabeth—the ship, not the monarch—and had a voice to match. She bellowed when I drew captioned cartoons about the teachers while she was trying to teach us the alphabet. I said, "I already know those letters. My Uncle Kelly taught me how to spell SCHLITZ." She gave me a narrow-eyed look and told my mother that afternoon, "You're going to have a lot of trouble with that child when she grows up. You better do something about it RIGHT NOW."

What they did was to take me out of Mrs. Snyder's and back to the kitchen table at Yaya's house, where Uncle Kelly proceeded with his own curriculum. It was thanks to him that I insulted Mrs. Katerini, the Greek lady who lived next door.

My parents' second apartment, which I remember even though we left it when I was three, had a long narrow hall with all rooms opening off it to the right. The hall led straight from the front door to the kitchen. It was in our kitchen that I confronted Mrs. Katerini.

Being younger than three, I was sitting in my wooden highchair as we ate supper. Mrs. Katerini came to the screened back door, looked in and saw us at the kitchen table. She said in Greek, "Oh, you're eating! I don't want to disturb you, I'll just wait out here till you're finished."

My father jumped up and opened the door, saying, "No, please, come in, Mrs. Katerini! Join us."

"No, no, I don't want a thing. Don't let me bother you, I'll just stand right outside here till you've finished."

"No, please, come in and join us at the table!"

"Oh, I wouldn't dream of it. I'll just . . . ."

At this moment, looking up from my baby dish, I called out a scatological phrase that defies translation in civilized company. Mrs. Katerini paled and went home. My father went out and bought me ice cream.

When I was three we moved to a country neighborhood called Ingleside. The wonderful house we bought reminded me of what I imagined Red Riding Hood would have lived in. It was Tudor-style, or what we called "Old English," pale stucco with dark brown trim, gables and many windows. It had huge yards, front and back, a fish pond and lots of trees. I'm told that the house was a shambles when we moved in because the former owners had been messy and tacky, but it was a dream come true for my mother, whose talents lay in fixing, repairing, decorating and rebuilding.

I loved the house, mainly because my mother adored it, and I did not notice for a moment that there were absolutely no children my age living nearby. This suited me fine because I got to play with Mama instead. She was older and considerably more mature than the children I had met up to that point, her nose didn't run and she didn't break my toys or say "Nyah, nyah."

Looking back on those years when I played with Mama instead of with other kids, I wonder how weary she must have gotten, stopping her sanding and painting and sewing, to watch me give puppet shows or to look at my cartoons. If she was annoyed she never showed it.

It occurs to me that the games I remember most fondly are the ones that never involved toys. The tall trees were already in our yard, and we had to eat lunch every day, so Mama thought of a way to combine these things that seemed far more interesting than any store full of dolls or games. I made up names for the trees, such as "Running Brook," "Indian Princess" or "Old Ironsides," the mighty oak by our front door. I wrote the names on two separate sets of labels and then, armed with straight pins and one set of labels, ran outside to pin them to the bark of the appropriate trees.

Indoors, Mama put the corresponding set of labels into a bowl and, as I watched excitedly, drew one. "Running Brook!" she might exclaim. And as we made sandwiches and wrapped cookies in waxed paper and stuffed eggs, I trembled in excitement, telling her, "Wait'll you see what tree it is! You're going to love it!"

And she would. She was the most enthusiastic person I ever met. I would guide her outdoors to Running Brook, the tall pine over by the corner of the front yard and, as I had anticipated, she would cry, "Oh, wonderful! I hoped it would be this one!" We would spread our cloth under Running Brook, on the soft, shiny bed of pine needles, and eat lunch and talk. I don't remember what we talked about but it wouldn't have been a problem, because Mama loved to talk and usually did so nonstop.

Once an irritable relative said to me, "My GOD, your mother talks a lot!" and I had to concede that it was true. But, given the choice between a silent, stone-faced parent and Mama, interrupting, analyzing and repeating, I would have chosen Mama.

3
DEVELOPING AN APPETITE

I started school at Ingleside Elementary on the outskirts of Norfolk. The school building was brick with white trim, tall and skinny with big, long windows, and it contained four large classrooms, two on each floor, a tiny principal's office and a damp basement with bathrooms in it that students nowadays would picket as unhygienic.

I had Miss Brosius for first and second grades. There were, in fact, two grades in every room and one teacher had to take care of both from nine A.M. until three P.M. In the middle of first grade, Miss Brosius became Mrs. Wooden and then had a baby, which was an exciting development that had us giggling and whispering behind our hands. I still know Mrs. Wooden and she looks exactly as I remember her from first grade and still has the same sense of humor. I had forgotten it, but she tells me that one boy in our class said proudly, "My daddy's a polar bear." When she asked him to explain this, he replied, "Well, see, his cousin died and he was one of the polar bears." When you taught two grades every day in one room, it was an advantage to have a couple of comedians in the class to ease the pain.

The teachers gave gold stars for good conduct, and I was one of the few who didn't get one during the first grading period. It was, Miss Brosius told my mother, because I wouldn't stop talking. Mama didn't protest. How could she? She knew where it came from.

We students had to bring our lunches from home, and this created an interesting challenge for a Greek-American family preoccupied with cuisine. Mama told Daddy, "Get Hope a lunch box for school." The other kids had little rectangular green-and-gray tin lunch boxes. My father went to a place where construction foremen bought their supplies and got me a huge, black lunch box shaped like a locomotive, with a quart-sized thermos and three compartments. The first day of school my parents put spaghetti with meat sauce in the thermos and filled the compartments with a slice of moussaka, a little salad in a dish with a jar of olive oil and vinegar, half a cheese sandwich, a banana and a slice of cake.

When I opened the locomotive in front of the other kids, they all fell around the floor holding their stomachs and gagging, "Yuk, yuk, YUK!" I cried at home that afternoon, and my mother asked, "What was in *their* lunches?"

"Peanumbutter and jelly samwiches with no crusts," I howled.

My mother said, "They're going to die of scurvy." I never complained again, although it was thirty years before I found out what scurvy was: I think you have to be a cabin boy on a whaler to get it.

Another outcome of starting school was finding out that there really were children living in my neighborhood, albeit many blocks away. So I developed friendships, if one could call them that. It didn't take long to figure out that these kids weren't as easy to get along with as Mama.

All I seem to remember from those years is hearing, "You said you were comin' to my house and you went to Phyllis' house and that's not fair because you said we were gonna play dolls and you lied and I'm gonna tell my mummuh to tell your mummuh." Kids were mean.

For some reason, all I could ever bring myself to reply to these diatribes was "Maybe you're right," the cowardly pacifist's response. Years later, after a lifetime of saying "Maybe you're right" to abrasive persons, I was told by a concerned friend that I ought to take an assertiveness course. I thought, "Maybe she's right." But I was afraid that if I took the course, I would begin sounding like the little girl who yelled at me for going to Phyllis' house. There are enough people in the world to be scared of without having to be scared of yourself too.

Fortunately, I had at the time another friend who could be an occasional buffer against some of the more possessive playmates, and that was Eldora—a wonderfully calm and good-natured young woman who came each day to help with house-keeping when I was nine years old. The first day she came to work, she and I went crabbing and brought home a bushel of blue crabs which we steamed for a dinner-time treat. Eldora has retired now, after giving me a hand in my household too when the kids were young, but she and I still go out for fried shrimp lunches and reminisce about the neighborhood kids, especially the ones she thought were bullies: "Lawd, that Phyllis got on my nerves."

Some of the children fought with their parents and siblings, which amazed me, an only child with no siblings for competition. My friend June and her sister Mildred had a loud, yelling row over the mayonnaise. Mildred kept putting it into the refrigerator and June kept yanking it back out, screaming, "It says right here on the jar: 'DON'T FREEZE.'" I was about eight years old, but I had figured out that there was a difference between refrigerating and freezing. I was, however, too much of a wimp to interrupt the fight, and something told me that becoming involved would work to my detriment. So I watched long-faced for a while and then slunk home, leaving them to throw mayonnaise around. This experience must have provided the subconscious warning flag that has subsequently prevented my entering politics or being on boards.

Even though I was in school and presumably suffering under a more restrictive regime, I still remembered the glories of show biz, as revealed to me when I stood on the kitchen table spelling beers. There were ample opportunities to develop this bent. When Mrs. Debnam suggested in fourth grade that we take turns reading aloud, I asked if we could write and perform a radio show.

Radio, of course, was the major medium of the time. There was no television yet and we didn't really need it, having all the visuals in our minds. We learned more valuable tidbits from the daily radio programs than you might imagine. I knew all the theme songs from the radio soap operas, and years later

I was stunned, when taking piano lessons, to find in a book of classical pieces the theme song for "Pepper Young's Family." It's "Au Matin" by Godard. Go look it up. And Camay soap was the sponsor.

I visualized Lorenzo Jones and his wife Belle, the protagonists of one favorite soap opera. Unquestionably, Lorenzo had to be skinny and sport a small moustache. And Front Page Farrell must certainly have looked like James Cagney and would have worn a hat all day long, even indoors at the newspaper office. And why, I wondered, didn't somebody on the script committee over at "One Man's Family" write a line other than "Yes, yes, Fanny," for Father Barber to say?

When we performed our radio show in the fourth grade, we actors piled into the Cloak Room, a sliding-door closet at the back of the classroom in which we kept our coats, galoshes and lunches. In muffled voices we broadcast our show from the depths of the Cloak Room, complete with commercials and sound effects, while everyone outside sitting at the little desks clapped and cheered. While we were broadcasting, we ate most of their lunches.

About this time I developed a healthy interest in eating well. At first this pleased my parents, who had worried greatly about my picky appetite and skinny body when I first began school. But by fourth grade I was wearing Chubbette dresses and dreaded desperately the day every few months when a public health nurse would arrive in the classroom, dragging behind her a doctor's scales on wheels. One by one, we had to go up to the front of the classroom to be weighed. It was humiliating enough to stand on the scales in front of thirty or forty whooping, snickering classmates, but the *coup de grace* was the nurse's method of recording the data. "Seventy-five!" or "Eighty-two!" she would shout to Mrs. Debnam, who would write it down on a chart next to the pupil's name.

"EIGHTY-TWO!" the class would echo joyously. "You're FAT!"

Yet I still looked forward to every meal, particularly since Daddy loved good cuisine and oversaw most of the menus. To a certain extent, food is a general obsession with Greeks anyway. Feeding others and eating heartily oneself were high priorities not only for my parents but for the entire extended family.

My maternal grandmother practically existed to cook and feed. She took it a little too far by avoiding as far as possible eating in other people's houses, making it clear that only her kitchen produced edible cuisine.

A force-feeding that became legendary in our family history concerned the visit to Yaya of Miz Wells, the second-grade teacher at Marshall Elementary School in Norfolk. It is important to remember that Yaya was the only woman of Greek descent living in Southeastern Virginia during her first six or seven years in the United States. Men had immigrated on and off, but my grandfather was the first to come to the area bringing a ready-made wife straight from the village with him from the start.

This meant that there was no one with whom Yaya could socialize in the United States except for her husband. If she had been back in the village, she would have received social calls from other young married women, and this would have given her the opportunity to show off her prowess in the kitchen, making the others feel insecure.

But there were no young married women in Norfolk who could speak Greek, and at first Yaya wasn't brave enough to tackle the language barrier at tea-time with Anglo-Saxon neighbors. Later, when she became friendly with them all, she never understood why they didn't rush to prepare party food the moment she entered their houses. I didn't understand it either when I went visiting with Yaya, and I embarrassed everyone by yelling in Mrs. Clough's house, "When is she going to bring out a tray?", which she never did.

And so Yaya kept busy at home having and raising babies and longing for a social visit, until her opportunity arose one day under combat conditions. My Aunt Connie had a fight with a boy in the second grade. He pulled her pigtail, and she hit him with a book. The teacher, Miz Wells, separated them and asked Aunt Connie, "Dawlin', what's your name again?"

Aunt Connie piped, "Connie Christopoulos."

"You're that little Grecian child, awn't you," said Miz Wells. "I want you to go tell your mama that I'm comin' over to see her this afternoon." Miz Wells wanted to be sure that the foreign family understood the proper tenets of child care and, presumably, nutrition.

Aunt Connie sped home after school like a meteor and announced the imminent arrival of Miz Wells. Yaya stood stunned for a minute and then realized, with a mixture of joy and terror, that her chance had finally come to stuff a stranger to death. She dashed into the kitchen and threw a pan of baklava into the oven, sliced some ham and several cheeses, filled a dish with black olives and put bread on to rise. This was to be the Main Serving.

And then she prepared the First Serving. You don't want to make a guest wait for the Main Serving; a tense wait during social conversation, of which she would in any case be incapable, would be intolerable and impolite. The First Serving, decreed by tradition, is homemade preserves, the best kind you have. You pile the preserves into a cut-glass bowl, put out a fork or spoon and a glass of cold water for every guest, and then—sort of in the rear of the tray—you place an assortment of cordials, liqueurs and wines in tiny glasses. The guest must pick up a utensil, take a helping of preserves and eat it over the water in case it drips, sip the water and then select the alcoholic beverage of his or her choice.

Yaya's preserves had come from Greece. It's hard to find preserved green walnuts unless you have easy access to walnut trees, because you have to cut the rascals off the trees early on, before they form shells, and then preserve them in a rich, thick, heavy, powerful syrup. One of them might last two weeks after you eat it.

In the proper and generous spirit of Greek Overkill, Yaya filled the cut-glass bowl to the brim because a Greek doesn't want to look stingy even if only one guest is expected. And then, at precisely 4:30, there was a knock at the door. Miz Wells stood there in her hat and long, dark coat and said, "Are you Miz Christolipus?"

Yaya said "SEET DOWN." She had learned a few phrases from the kids.

Miz Wells was nervous. She sat right by the front door in a straight chair, keeping on her coat and hat. Yaya ran to the kitchen without another word and brought back the First Serving. She held the tray a few inches from the teacher's chin and yelled (because you always talk louder to foreigners), "EAT!!"

Like a good Virginian, Miz Wells simpered, "Well, now, ah doan know if ah can eat all this, but ah certny will try." And, unaware of proper procedure, she lifted the heavy bowl off the tray, picked up her fork, and ate all eighteen of the preserved green walnuts.

Yaya watched the precious morsels disappear down Miz Wells' gullet and pondered how to intervene and explain the custom of one per person. But you can't interrupt an orgy. And besides, the Greeks bring it on themselves by putting out too big a helping in the first place for show-off purposes.

Miz Wells was woozy by the time she had finished the bowl. She reached for the water and then spotted the liqueur glasses. "Mercy, what's in all these li'l glasses?"

Down went the ouzo. Then the seven-star Metaxa brandy. She knocked off the wild cherry wine and then killed the pear cordial. By the time she had finished all eight, she had forgotten the reason for the visit and had to be guided to the door. It was the last time Yaya saw Miz Wells. The old girl survived, but Yaya wasn't about to return the visit by going to a PTA meeting, a concept as totally foreign to her as preserved green walnuts in a bowl might be to the Marshall School faculty.

The wild cherry wine on that tray, incidentally, was a vitally important part of the Christopoulos family's heritage and lifestyle. Yaya, the daughter of a wine maker, had learned the subtle tricks and secrets of the trade. Her homemade wines were a wonderful staple on the family table at every dinner.

We still have the pungent barrels and wooden presses that she used, but nobody can duplicate the recipes. How could we? When Yaya got ready to make wine, she would send one of her children to the store for a bunch of grapes. When the "test" bunch was brought home, Yaya would grasp a grape and mash it between her thumb and forefinger. "Yes, these okay," she would say, and back would go the kids to buy a crate of the fruit.

The finger test also told her how much sugar to use. Her youngest son, Chris, was interested in cooking and viticulture and tried to write down the wine recipe as she worked. Having measured and recorded the amounts of fruit and sugar, he watched in dismay a few months later as she started a second batch. After mashing a grape, Yaya muttered, "Only one bag sugar this time."

"But it was two and a half last time, Mamaki!"

"These different grapes," she said with finality.

The barrels lent a wonderfully resinous taste to the wines, and our favorite was the wild cherry, which she made from trees on the lawn of the beach house. On the wall of the den in my own family home is the framed front page of the *Norfolk Ledger-Dispatch* for October 12, 1926. Its place of honor on our wall is due to the wild cherry wine.

During Prohibition, Yaya continued to make her good wine and to store it in barrels in the big cellar of the family's city house on Colonial Avenue in Norfolk. One summer while the family was at the beach house, the neighborhood policeman on his Colonial Avenue beat noticed a light burning in the cellar of the Christopoulos house. Knowing that the family was away, he suspected an intruder and, with the key that Papou had left him for security, let himself in and went down to the cellar. The rows of barrels and the exhilarating smell of fermenting fruit impressed the good officer, so much so that he suddenly remembered Prohibition and decided that the contents of the cellar were illegal. He summoned a paddy wagon to confiscate the goods and have them removed to the police station.

The next day a small article in the local section of the paper announced the bust of the Christopoulos wine cellar. Papou was devastated. He was an honorable man, he shouted rhetorically to the assembled family members, an honest, dedicated resident of the great United States, a respecter of its laws! And now, to be branded a common criminal in the newspaper! He contemplated either suicide or a return to Greece.

My mother had been reading the papers too, and she suddenly remembered an article some months before, outlining the regulations of Prohibition. "Papa," she cried, "we didn't do anything wrong! The law says you can make wine from fruit on your property."

"You're sure? Come on, we're going to City Hall."

Father and daughter took the streetcar to town and looked up the statute. My mother was right. Armed with this vital information, Papou and his youngest daughter stormed the police station. "I want my wine back!" Papou thundered, his black eyes sparkling and handle-bar moustache quivering.

"Now, George, be reasonable," said the police captain. "You broke the law." "I did NOT!" And Papou revealed the disclaimer in the national law. "And not only do I want my wine back today," Papou continued, "I want a headline on the FRONT PAGE of the *Ledger-Dispatch* to say that I am not a criminal."

On the front of the October 12 edition, just under stories about Al Capone and the visiting Queen of Romania, is a headline trumpeting "CHRISTOPOULOS WINE RETURNED."

4

A BLEND OF CULTURES

It was a good thing that my appetite had improved by the time I was eleven, because that year we went to Cyprus to meet my father's relatives. On the way to Cyprus aboard the S.S. Vulcania, I caught measles. My mother said it was Those Missionary Children we met on board: she had suspected them all along of being up to no good. But before the incubation period was over and the measles actually sprang forth, I managed to have a pretty good time at our first stop, Egypt. We spent a week there, and even though something about it scared me, I still understood the glamour of it. What scared me was the disorder and confusion and yelling, the outstretched palms and shouts of "Baksheesh!" which we learned at once meant "Tip!", "Money!" or "Buddy, can you spare a dime?" In addition, the goats, chickens, camels, heat and flies were all new companions to us on city streets. Perhaps, we realized a few years later, it had been the flies and not the wretched missionary kids which had been responsible for my measles.

I rode a camel at the Pyramids, so my father could take a picture of me, and you can tell from the expression on my face in the photo that it made me motion sick and the camel smelled funny. Now that I have done it once, I see no reason ever to do it again.

The measles came out once we were on the little boat from Alexandria to Cyprus, and Mama treated me secretly, in collusion with the ship's doctor, who told us it was surely scarlet fever but that, if I could keep from coughing or gagging, I could be sneaked off the ship after all in Cyprus so that he wouldn't have to report the disease and quarantine everybody on board for two weeks.

The effort to keep from coughing as we went through customs made me stand about with my cheeks puffed out and eyes crossed, but apparently people thought this normal for an

American child. And the Cypriot relatives, who had never seen me before, loved me anyway as only Greeks and Cypriots can love relatives—eagerly, joyously, hugging and kissing, giving up every comfort or pleasure of their own to make it mine.

I got the best room in the big, cool, beautiful house, a house that had huge, high-ceilinged rooms that opened onto a courtyard with flagstone floors and gardens full of kumquat and jasmine and love-apple trees. And because I had the measles, they treated me with the time-honored cure-all Invalid's Diet of Cyprus: plain boiled rice, seasoned with lemon juice and a pinch of salt. I ate this three times a day for almost a week, until the family doctor looked me over and said I could get dressed and come down next day for dinner. We had homemade ravioli in chicken broth. I remember every bite I took, every nuance of flavor, and I remember picking up the plate after asking permission, to lick up the remaining sauce.

By the time I came down to that first dinner, I had learned Greek. I played games and cards every day in my sickroom with my two young cousins, who didn't speak a word of English. Just as I had learned to read and spell English by memorizing beer brands, I learned Greek by memorizing the words for Jack, Queen, King and Ace.

We stayed in Cyprus for six months, and Daddy bought a tiny English car which we drove all over the island. Being Americans, we thought little of picking up in the morning and driving fifty or sixty miles across the entire length of the country. The Cypriot relatives were aghast. For a trip of this magnitude they packed lunches and brought blankets and pillows.

We swam in the Mediterranean, which was warm, shallow, salty and clean. And we went to a picnic one night that I will never forget. It's been a long time, but I still remember everything we ate—not unusual for me, alas—and nearly everything we did.

The picnic spot was a fig tree grove up in the mountains at a town called Pyrgos, which means tower. The ruined tower of a medieval fortress stood nearby. By the time we arrived in midafternoon, men and boys had been roasting whole suckling pigs since morning over open wood fires, turning them slowly all the time on long wooden spits as grease spattered the embers and caused little flickers of blue and orange flame to leap up. The aroma greeted us as we got out of our little English Ford further down the mountain.

I don't remember exactly who was giving the picnic and providing the food, but a good-sized group of village women, wearing aprons and bandannas, had set up long tables under the Grandfather Fig Tree. They told us it was a 300-stake tree. This meant that it had grown so big and its branches were so heavy with fruit that as many as 300 stakes had to be driven into the ground beneath it here and there so that the branches might rest on them for support.

There was a cold stream running beside the table. The women had put tomatoes and cucumbers and jugs of wine in it to get cold. After we sat down, they brought the heavy, dark round loaves of bread Cypriots used to bake each day in domed adobe ovens in their back yards. These days, most of them get white sliced bread from the bakery. Along with the vegetables and bread came chunks of sharp cheese.

As it started getting dark and the moon began to rise, the first of the pigs was taken off the spit and carved and carried on huge wooden boards to the table. The pigs had been stuffed with rice, pine nuts and raisins, and the stuffing was piled in steaming mounds on the boards next to the pork.

Eating was raucous and festive and went on for a very long time. When the table had finally been cleared of meat and vegetables, watermelons and figs, cold from the icy stream, were brought to replace them. What was there left to do, finally, after all the eating? Sing, that's what, and after the Cypriots had gone through their repertoire of folk songs, someone asked my mother to sing something American. She was stumped for a minute and then she remembered two songs on which she and I could harmonize—"Old Black Joe" and "Silent Night." We had to repeat both of them several times, while our Cypriot hosts clinked glasses and wiped away tears of emotion. Oblivious of any racial connotations, every Greek I have ever met adores "Old Black Joe." In fact, my Norfolk Yaya had left word that it be sung at her funeral, which it was.

We brought my father's mother back to America with us at the conclusion of our Cyprus trip. It was not a good idea in the long run, because the witty, spunky old lady was used to her Cypriot social life, which involved afternoon tea, card games, cigarettes, and perpetual visiting and strolling.

In our quiet suburban Virginia neighborhood, she was bored silly. And when we took her to call on other Greek women in Norfolk, she was bored even sillier, and they were scandalized by her worldliness. Worse, she and my father shouted wildly at one another—just as June and Mildred had battled over the mayonnaise—and the household arguments were a terrifying new experience. Because Daddy thought his mother was difficult, unreasonable and frivolous, I thought so too and wished she hadn't come. It was not until years later, long after she had gone back—and it didn't take her long—that I realized how interesting and, in fact, how charming she had been. But that's the way it often is with people who do things a little differently from the crowd. Cypriot Yaya didn't just march to a different drummer; she stampeded. She was fun, and I didn't realize it.

Our neighbors in suburban Ingleside had been charmed by Cypriot Yaya. They were marvelous people themselves—solid, intelligent, people of quality and warmth. Almost everybody in the neighborhood attended Ingleside Presbyterian Church, a small brick building of age and grace, with a pastor of legendary wisdom, Dr. W.H.T. Squires. After his death, they renamed the church Squires Memorial in tribute to him. Even though we were Greek Orthodox and had to travel all the way downtown to church, I joined my Ingleside playmates at the Presbyterian Sunday School and Junior Choir.

Most beguiling of all was Vacation Bible School. On mild summer mornings we would all troop into the church social hall and separate into teams. One year we were the Cherokees and the Chuckatucks, and we tried to outdo each other in winning points. How we achieved the points I haven't the slightest idea, but I know that we won the cheering contest because of a cheer I had made up:

> Strawberry icing, chocolate cake!
> Cherokee is just a fake.
> Don't you worry, don't you fret,
> Chuckatuck is the best team yet!

About that time I became enamored of the hymns. Roy Brinkley Sr., the Sunday School superintendent, was a big, tall, heavy man with a trilly, high-pitched voice. He harmonized splendidly on such numbers as: "A volunteer for Jesus, a soldier true! Jesus is the captain, we're the crew!" The harmony was even better in other hymns:

> *I was sinking deep in sin, far from the peaceful shore,*
> *Sinking, sinking, deep within, sinking to rise no more,*
> *When the master of the seas heard my despairing cry,*
> *From the waters lifted me, and saved was I!*
> *Love lifted me, love lifted me,*
> *When nothing else could help, love lifted me!*

Mr. Brinkley dragged out those last three words in heart-rending, gospel-style harmony, and I was blown away. This kind of singing was heady stuff to a Greek Orthodox kid whose only experience with church singing so far had been the nasal chanters and a few Kyrie Eleisons from the choir. It made me think seriously, at age eleven, of joining Ingleside Presbyterian. All my playmates jumped up and down in delight at this possibility, and I told my parents one night at dinner that this was what I wanted to do.

Like the good parents they were, they sat worriedly together that evening and all the next day to discuss it. Surely in so serious a matter they could not and would not stand in my way. They told me that if this was indeed what I wished, I could join the Presbyterian Church. I ran off, half-worried and half-elated, to tell my friends. The next afternoon, dignified old Dr. Squires came to call. I was out playing, but it was my parents he wanted to see. "While we would love to have Hope in our congregation," he said, "may I ask that you tell her to wait a few years before making a decision of this magnitude? You have a very fine church of your own, and she may come to prefer it later on. Just now she wants to be with her little friends."

He was right. By the time I was fourteen, I had begun to play the organ at the old Greek church downtown and was moved and fascinated by the Byzantine music and ritual and the ethnic familiarity of the church community. This incident convinced our family that Dr. Squires was probably one of the wisest Christian clergymen we had ever met.

That same year, 1950, Rudolf Bing became general manager of the Metropolitan Opera Company in New York. I didn't know much about Rudolf Bing, but I was already an opera fan just from listening to the Met broadcasts on Saturday afternoons. This interest had come about because my father, who knew nothing about music and didn't particularly care to find out, had heard opera years before when he was a college student in Greece. He had liked it and admired the sound of the human voice. One day somewhere downtown he caught sight of records for sale and brought home two of them because he had heard of the opera selections on them—the *Rigoletto* quartet, a *Traviata* duet, and the sextet from *Lucia di Lammermoor*. He put on the scratchy old 78's, sat back in his chair, closed his eyes contentedly and said, "Now, THIS is music!" I was impressed. Daddy had never before said that about any piece of music. He didn't know what the Star-Spangled Banner sounded like and couldn't care less. His enthusiasm for opera was contagious.

I remember thinking dreamily in the early '50s that if ever the unimaginable should occur and I should someday have to get a job, the only thing I would really like to do would be work for Rudolf Bing, who had just been publicized as the new general manager of the Metropolitan Opera. It was a fantasy, rather like winning the lottery, and I put it out of my mind the moment I thought of it.

At that point, my involvement with music was limited to the Greek Church organ, a volunteer job that was the result of eight years of piano lessons with the brilliant and terrifying Bristow Hardin, one of Virginia's most distinguished piano teachers. He had noted my ability to play by ear (Uncle Kelly had made me play "Oh, Susanna" over and over) and took me on as a pupil, scaring the devil out of me for the next eight years.

He had every reason to be hard on me: I never practiced. Probably I felt somehow that lots of practice would mean this was serious business, and I didn't want to be a serious pianist. Playing in public for an attentive audience I deemed frightening beyond belief.

People who fear speaking in public find it interesting that I feared piano recitals but have no qualms about addressing an audience of hundreds with no notes. It seems to me the obvious difference is that you can ad lib when speaking but you don't mess around with Mozart. Either you play it right or not at all.

5
DISCOVERING ACADEMIA

I attended Miss Turnbull's School in Norfolk from sixth grade through high school. Miss Turnbull was brilliant and eccentric, a spinster who had shocked everyone in Norfolk in 1921 by going to Vassar and graduating Phi Beta Kappa. She figured the best thing she could do for women after that was start a girls' school and introduce them to the intellectual wonders of the world.

There were only forty-five of us in the entire school at Miss Turnbull's those years. The ratio of teacher to student was occasionally 1:2. We studied English in phenomenal depth, ancient and European history, Latin and French. On a less exalted plane we took mathematics, and as for science, Miss T. did not particularly like it but she was aware that we needed at least a year of it for college entrance.

Consequently every third year she offered biology, to pacify the colleges. Our laboratory, where we dissected frogs and studied cells, was also the lunchroom, a circumstance which developed iron stomachs even in the most naturally queasy.

We also gave plays all the time, classics and one-acts, made up irreverent skits at recess, performed in musical satires that Miss Turnbull herself wrote for the annual luncheon and acted out great scenes of literature for class assignments. I had to play Henry VIII and acted fat and wore a glued-on beard and threw chicken bones over my shoulder. If it had been a co-ed school, an experience of this profundity might never have come my way.

It occurred to me around age fifteen that I might want to go out of state to college. Everybody I had ever met up to that point had stayed close to home. Miss T.'s graduates went to Vassar, Wellesley, Bryn Mawr and Smith. If they stayed in Virginia, they chose Sweet Briar and Hollins. And everyone almost always majored in liberal arts. Now when we alumnae read newspapers and magazines we get downright ugly when we spot grammatical errors and incorrect historical data.

One fall Miss Turnbull hired a one-year-only biology teacher, a nice young woman from North Carolina who probably knew her biology but had a good old Southern problem with the pronunciation of foreign-sounding terms. When we studied insect species, for example, she pronounced arachnida "archa-nider," and insisted on saying lar-nix and phar-nix for larynx and pharynx. A lot of people continue to do this and I do think it's a Southern problem, which I suppose is all right for me to say because I too am Southern. In fact, I saw LARNYX written prominently in a North Carolina newspaper headline recently.

We got irritated at the mispronunciations, and two of the braver girls in the class proposed that the next time she said lar-nix we should all throw our books on the floor. Most people did. I got cowardly and only threw a pencil, but the teacher got the idea that something was amiss and snapped, "You-all just think you're SO SMART, don't you? What do you think you're makin' all that racket for?"

My friend Grace said, "We get mad when you say lar-nix instead of larynx."

The teacher said, "What makes you think you kin pronounce lar-nix right if you never even had biology before?"

There was only so much blackboard jungle in us and we gave up, managing to slither past the science section of the college boards to get into college on the strength of the verbal scores. To this day most of us have not the remotest idea what a larynx actually is.

"Ah don't know why in the WORRUL you're sendin' her nawth to college," a neighbor told my mother. "They're not like us up theah. They're right snooty." But they weren't, they were just like everybody else and they were nice, too. When I arrived as a freshman at Vassar College in Poughkeepsie, New York, I found that southerners were in the minority. They still are. Offhand I can remember four or five girls from the south in our class. People were polite and didn't tease us about our accents, but we felt dumb.

Girls from Pennsylvania and Minnesota answered questions in elegant intellectual jargon, or perhaps it seemed intellectual to me because they pronounced their R's. After all, when someone responds to a professor by saying, "I prefer to analyze this problem further before making a definitive statement" in a Midwestern accent, it sounds a heck of a lot smarter than having some southerner mumble, "Ah rully doan know, sir."

But soon we realized that we southerners were harder on ourselves than the non-southerners were on us. They listened, nodding, to our opinions, they voted for us in campus elections, they laughed at our jokes. And the professors even wrote things on our papers such as "Very good. You have shown original thought." I suspected that our incredible naivete so stunned them they had no choice but to consider it original.

I liked college and thought the other girls were friendly. Nobody seemed to care what anybody wore at Vassar, which would have been a shock to the Norfolk saleswomen and my Aunt Connie, who made my precollege shopping trips a veritable Hell, warning that They weren't wearing That and you had to wear what They did or They would look at you sideways and whisper.

The classes were excellent and small so that we got to know our professors well. Some of them, even ones whose courses I never took, are close friends to this day, especially Winifred Asprey of the Math Department. I stay with her whenever I visit Vassar, which means she has to lay in an extraordinary supply of food and drink to accommodate me and the legions of retired faculty who come over to visit and reminisce while I'm there.

Although some students knew from the start what their major fields would be, I agonized over it, making wrong, desperate decisions, confused by the smorgasbord of tempting departments and good professors. At first, being a ham of long standing, I was smitten by the drama department. But then I took the introductory theater course and was struck dumb with terror by the legendary Miss Heinlein, the department head and a stage director of great temperament. She lost her temper during rehearsals in unique new ways. Also, it was clear that a substantial part of a drama major's time, both in and out of class, might naturally be spent painting and building sets, designing costumes and rehearsing lines.

Lacking sufficient theatrical motivation to consider giving up celebrated courses in English, French, music and classics to do what I could do less professionally in the extracurricular student shows, I slunk into Miss Heinlein's office to tell her I had changed my mind about being a drama major. Miss Heinlein was, as always, wearing a severe suit and health shoes, her white hair cropped short, eyes cool behind glasses, and her facial expressions changed rapidly from warm and cordial to grim and steely, just the way her voice did during rehearsals.

"Someday, Hope," she told me in a measured, trembling whisper, building slowly in a crescendo to a tone that bounced off the office walls, "you'll start to peel apart the layers of your personality, just the way. . . JUST THE WAY. . .one peels the skin off an onion. Peeeeel, peel, SLOWLY, looking for the core. . . And, just as in an onion, THERE WILL BE NO CORE."

By now I was perspiring heavily. For want of a more articulate defense, I reverted to the old Phyllis Phrase of childhood: "Maybe you're right."

"I'm afraid I AM right." Whisper again. "Go back and tell your adviser, your *English professor adviser*, that you want THAT CORE. That you have a talent that could FORM THAT CORE."

I went stumbling blindly in fear straight to my adviser's office to tell him that I had decided to major in English, peels and cores notwithstanding. And not only did I choose English, I chose the area of English that most of the numerous other English majors avoided—Medieval Studies.

How could people have avoided that subject? The best course I ever took was Miss Giffin's senior seminar in Medieval Romance. The kids in Contemporary Press and Creative

Writing laughed at us derisively, the five of us sitting happily around a wooden table in a distant, windowless room in the library, listening to words of wit and intellect from a woman who resembled a medieval study herself.

Miss Giffin was short and shapeless, wore proper tweed suits and sensible shoes, and had pale red hair and a pale reddish complexion. She resembled a cheerful roseate tomato. But her eyes twinkled, and when she talked, her chin jutted out like Elsa Lanchester's. She always wore a hopeful smile, and her eternal academic optimism made her find something of value in anything a student said.

"Miss Giffin, I didn't finish the term paper because the Glee Club went to Yale."

"Ah, the Glee Club! Do you know the derivation of the term 'glee club'? An examination of the Oxford English Dictionary might reveal that 'glee' is of Anglo-Saxon origin. However in medieval times . . ."

You could do no wrong.

Despite her supposedly stuffy specialty, Miss Giffin was happily aware of the passions and scandals of the Middle Ages and enjoyed discussing them matter-of-factly in the classroom. And if her tweediness seemed old-fashioned, a visit to her apartment for dinner could prove a revelation. Her place was decorated all in white—modern, overstuffed furniture, carpets, lamps, everything as white as the polar ice cap, except for her paintings, which were huge, modern, abstract splashes of red and green. She also served excellent wines along with the medieval dishes she had researched and learned to prepare in a contemporary manner.

Another nice thing about Vassar was that it was still a woman's college. For late social bloomers it was a blessing not to be thrown drastically in those nervous times into classrooms with men who might raise one eyebrow and not laugh if you said something funny. My daughters tell me now that in some ways they envy me for having gone to an all-woman college, where there is less pressure on one for serious intimate romances just because everybody else has them. It would appear that for some the supposed liberation of the sixties led to even greater entrapments.

But we didn't think of romance as entrapment in those days, there being such a scarcity of it. Some girls had boyfriends at the all-male colleges and were adept at cultivating more and more romances. Others of us were such late bloomers that they could have named us Aster. I went dutifully to mixers, where we girls were given numbers on pieces of paper and then told to stand in line rather like cows at a 4-H show while boys came forward to match their numbers with ours. Often one would spot a youth, generally one's own prospective date, trading numbers feverishly with other guys.

At my first mixer, a Yale football weekend, I was paired with Mike Nassau, a good-natured person who told me right off that he would never ask me out again because I wasn't Jewish and then refused to let anyone cut in on us when we danced because I was his date.

One or two similar experiences sophomore year led me to the conviction that it was unnecessary to go out on dates at all in college. No doubt, I surmised, there would be a few single men left in the world when I graduated. Until such time there was plenty of campus activity, albeit of an academic rather than a romantic nature, to distract me. Even though I wasn't the only person to come to this conclusion, social pressure was still rampant. Display of engagement rings in the dormitory dining room had reached fever pitch by the winter of our senior year and I could not help but feel insecure without one.

Then, unexpectedly, I achieved high-class social status among my peers because of Aunt Cleo the Matchmaker in Cyprus. Her cousin's son had seen my picture. This was not surprising because my father had ordered 200 wallet-size prints of the senior yearbook picture and had sent them all over the universe.

The prospective bridegroom, whose name was Doros, wanted all the necessary marital arrangements completed at once.

My father wrote Aunt Cleo that this was America and couples here made their own decisions; he was staying out of it. So Doros wrote me himself, in Greek, taking pains to mention that he stood to inherit his father's gravel company and Alfa-Romeo dealership and that I could choose any color car I wanted if I came to Cyprus that summer.

Immediately I became the envy of the Vassar campus. "GOD, Hopie, this is SEW roMANtic!" crowed my friends. "You absolutely MUST go this summer, really!"

How could this sedate yearbook picture have triggered such violent matchmaking?

But nagging fears intensified with Doros' third letter, in which he reported that what he loved most in life was to play cards, drink, and be entertained by the hostesses at all the Nicosia night spots, after which he would tool around the mountains in his Alfa Romeo at 125 kilometers an hour. He suggested that his plan in life was to continue this lifestyle and he hoped I would have my own little interests. What were they, by the way?

All grinning, bobbing, and eager, I wrote back in English that I liked Chaucer and opera. It took him a while to comprehend this. After an appreciable hiatus, along came an irritable letter in which he said there had been enough discussion of foolish little facts and he was ready to finalize the documents with my father.

I remembered the 125 kmh and said no.

It was only then that my father mentioned the fact that Doros' written Greek hovered somewhere around the fourth-grade level. "And you didn't tell me this?" I cried. No wonder I had enjoyed the wretched libertine's letters. Since my own written Greek is at a third-grade level, I felt like an intellectual giant because I could understand everything he wrote.

My rejection of this lucrative offer caused an international incident. Aunt Cleo wrote one brief, bitter note to Daddy and he never heard from her again. Families stopped speaking. A few duels were contemplated.

Only once again, years later, did I deal with a Cypriot matchmaker. This time it was the young man's mother herself, a lovely woman I had met on a trip to Cyprus in my working-girl days. She wanted me to marry her son, who was in graduate school in the United States. I met him and thought him bright and charming but, for some contrary reason, decided I did not want to marry him. NEVER LEARNING MY LESSON, I repeated the old pattern of writing to Cyprus in English while she responded in Greek. In a burst of creative vocabulary, I wrote the poor woman that while I admired her son greatly I could not contemplate marriage because "it's just a matter of chemistry." She thought he had failed his Wassermann test. Another international incident.

And so as senior year ended, I was still single—not an auspicious situation in 1956. Indeed, true social self-confidence did not develop until I was working in New York a year or so later. My inexperience was still remarkable when a group of graduate students came down to New York from New Haven to visit one of my apartment roommates. I was paired off in our wanderings around the east side with a blond, crew-cut quarterback.

He was good-natured and cheerful and thoroughly non-threatening. Suddenly he pulled me into a doorway somewhere down on Third Avenue and tried to kiss me. From old Greek upbringing habit, I pulled away and said, "No, no!" He was confused. "Why?" he asked.

My mind went blank. Why, indeed? I couldn't remember an appropriate answer, so I decided for once to tell the truth. "Because I don't think I'm a good kisser. I haven't done it that much and I don't know how."

He stared at me. "You don't know HOW?" "I mean it. I don't know what to do with my mouth and nose. Am I supposed to turn my head sideways? How do you breathe? Do you wet your lips first? Suppose I have garlic breath? See what I mean? I just don't think I do it right, and I'd really hate to disappoint you."

"Wait a minute," he said earnestly. "Let's just try it and I'll tell you if you're doing it right."

A quick smack, nothing Hollywoody or anything, more like sixth grade post office. "That was GOOD!" he cried encouragingly. "Now, maybe you could lean forward like this a little."

The romantic doorway interlude lasted maybe five or six minutes and then the others came to look for us, shouting, "Where have you two BEEN?" I felt like Colette or Lili Marlene. I never saw the Kissing Coach again after that evening, but it didn't matter. His roommate wrote to one of the other girls that Steve had sent me his best wishes and pronounced me one of the more honest, or possibly confusing, women he had ever met.

6
XXX-RATED JOB

Like many female college graduates of the mid-fifties, I had no plans whatsoever for a job or a career. We were supposed to find husbands as quickly as possible and let them worry about supporting us. Not only that, we never sought jobs in fields remotely related to the subjects we had majored in. Biology majors worked at publishing companies. Child Study majors became secretaries in insurance firms. Economics majors taught kindergarten. Being an English major, I wanted to work in opera.

But first I came home for a few months, thinking I might find a job while living comfortably with my family and eating home-cooked meals. My mother said one morning as I buttered a second piece of toast around eleven, "Maybe you can teach school."

I said, "How could I teach school? I never did the required reading in college. Suppose some kid asks me a question?"

My mother was obviously interested in getting me out of the house. "Listen, they would be dying to get you in the public schools. You have an English degree from Vassar."

The schools wouldn't touch me because I hadn't taken education courses. It was at this point that I mumbled, "I sort of hoped I could do something in an opera house." Such as brew coffee, I thought, or dust music stands.

My mother said, "Then, maybe you should go to some other city."

At the time I was amazed by this but didn't say so. I thought she was trying to force me out of town, my own mother—the one who loved me so much as her only child and with whom I had such fun doing things! Now I see what a courageous thing Mama was doing. Having been a daughter herself in a strict Greek family which wouldn't let her go fifty miles out of town to art school, she wanted me out of the way before the Find-a-Husband pressure began, both from my father, who was incited by the other Greek fathers in his social circle, and from my grandmother and her obedient household.

Besides, my grandmother thought—and said so often—that ONLY HOYDENS AND TRAMPS left the bosoms of their families and went off to live lives of dissipation in other cities. My mother had spunk. She could hardly wait for Grandmother to get upset about my going off to Sodom and Gomorrah, even if she would have to bear the brunt of it all as middlewoman.

And so, I joined my Vassar roommates in a tiny Bohemian-looking garret apartment in Cambridge, Massachusetts. I loved the neighborhood's charm and spirit. Since then the Cambridge city fathers have torn down the quaint houses in that area and put up giant, rich, ugly buildings for corporations that pay lots of taxes.

We lived on the third floor of an old frame house at 12 Story Street near Harvard Square. The landlady lived on the first floor, and an earnest, woodsy young couple who wore L.L.Bean boots and had two terrifying Dobermans lived on the second floor. We had to pass their landing to get to our apartment, and each time the dogs barked viciously behind the door, scrambling wildly, their nails rat-tat-tatting like machine-gun fire on the linoleum.

Ayla Karajabey, the Turkish roommate, was studying architecture at Harvard and is now a successful city planner in Istanbul. Joan Barton was taking musicology and now runs a fine tree farm on her family property in Vermont, the one job of all of ours that I envy the most. Kathy Brandt was getting a doctorate in art history from Harvard and is now a distinguished professor at NYU and consultant to the Vatican Museums for the conservation of the Sistine Chapel ceilings. I looked for a job in the yellow pages.

Somewhere I had read that you could find anything you wanted in the yellow pages, so I tried "Opera." Oddly, there was no such category. But they did list Musical Organizations. I began to dial the numbers, hoping some symphony conductor might hire me to make sandwiches for rehearsals.

When I reached the listing for the New England Conservatory of Music, I got lucky. The pleasant switchboard operator said, "You're interested in opera? Call Boris Goldovsky."

To tell an opera lover to call Boris Goldovsky was rather like advising a sports fan to dial Vince Lombardi. For years I had listened to Mr. Goldovsky's oddly-accented Russian voice on the Metropolitan Opera broadcast intermission features. He was famous.

"How do I get his phone number?"

"He's listed in the phone book."

Listed in the phone book. A man famous in his field who didn't consider himself too important to be listed. I knew immediately that this unpretentious man might be a person for whom I could work. I looked up his number.

Goldovsky himself answered the phone, stunning me. I spoke in a high-pitched quaver bordering on hysteria. "Mr. Goldovsky, my name is Hope Christopoulos and I just graduated from Vassar College and I majored in English and I'd like a job in opera, but I don't sing. I play the piano but you don't want to hear it. I speak Greek and French and I'm learning Italian, and I can type ten words a minute."

The only thing he noticed was the last phrase. "You type? I have just lost a series of secretaries. Come out tomorrow for an interview."

The next day I took the trolley to Brookline. Trembling with fear, I knocked on the door of his modest stucco house. His wife answered, and I saw children and a dog cavorting through the house, all of which made me feel better—until I spotted Goldovsky himself. He was wearing a morning coat, a waistcoat, and striped trousers. Ye gods, I thought, he dresses this way at home. Later I learned that he had just come from a lecture-recital; usually he wore short-sleeved sport shirts and baggy old pants. He was balding and fair and had a distant, absent-minded air about him.

He looked at his mail as he interviewed me and hardly ever glanced at my face. "What can you do?" he asked.

I repeated the credentials I had listed over the phone. Then he looked at me for the first time. "I think I know the job you want."

"What's that, sir?"

"You want my job."

Well, I thought, let's face it. "Yes, I do want a job like yours."

He smiled at last, somewhat resignedly. "My dear, do not think I am being sarcastic. I meant what I said. When I was your age, I wanted a job like mine too—head of an opera company, distinguished lecturer, orchestra conductor, pianist and coach, stage director. But, like you, I could do absolutely nothing."

He paused dramatically. "And so, I did the only thing I could possibly do. I made myself useful to a famous person. I am now famous. I need a slave. I need someone to do all the boring, stupid, tedious things I no longer have time to do. Do you want to be my slave?"

I didn't hesitate. It was 1957 and Slave was not an unusual job description for a female college graduate. "Yes sir," I said.

"A dollar twenty-five an hour," he murmured. "Take a letter."

I reached for a note pad and pencil. He watched me with a long-suffering smile. "Why do you take pencil and paper? Do you know shorthand?"

"No sir."

"Then why waste my time with longhand? Sit at the typewriter."

This was an unexpected trauma. "You want me to type as you *dictate?*"

"Well, what else can we do? It's your only skill. 'Dear Ralph.'"

I typed a small d, two spaces, then a capital EAR. This was before the days of self-correcting typewriters, so I reached for an eraser. It was at this moment that I learned I had stumbled upon the best boss in the world.

He said, "Why do you take an eraser?"

"I typed a mistake."

Goldovsky nodded and was silent for a moment. "Let me explain something to you. When you make a mistake and then you take the eraser and rub it out and go WHOOOOSH and blow away the little pieces of eraser, isn't it possible for the person who receives this letter to SEE that you erased and typed again? Is this not visible to the reader?"

"Yes," I conceded, "you would be able to see what I erased if you really looked."

"Then what you are doing is pretending to have typed perfectly, when any fool can see that you did not, isn't that right? Why do you want to LIE to the person who receives your letter? ADMIT your mistake. Put XXX through the word."

I had never thought of this logic before. He was absolutely right. I XXX-ed through the mistake and we went on. Every time I tried to outthink him as he dictated, I made a mistake and duly XXX-ed it out. When the letter was finished, I handed it to him. It had 876 X's in it.

Goldovsky said, "The typing is not terribly good. But the spelling is correct." AHA, I was an English major and, what was more, an opera lover. When he had dictated words like "tessitura" or "Goetterdaemmerung," I had taken my time and typed those correctly. It was things like "the," "and" and "but" that had given me trouble.

"Very well then, I won't have to waste time teaching you terminology," he said. "Put this in an envelope and mail it to Ralph Hunter. . ."

"Wait a minute, Mr. Goldovsky," I interrupted. "This letter is full of XXX's. Don't you want me to type it again?"

"My dear," he crooned, "people know I am an opera producer, but they don't know I have a secretary. They think I type my own letters. Why should I be a perfect typist? I am an artist. Send the letter."

Years later, after I had been working for some time in the world of opera, I would on occasion visit people well known in the field. From time to time I would see, framed and hanging on a wall, a letter I had typed.

I was Mr. Goldovsky's secretary and Girl Friday for the next year and a half. In terms of career, these were the most important eighteen months of my life because when I first went to work for Mr. G., I knew virtually nothing about opera except for what I had heard on the radio. By the time I left him for my next job, I had read, studied, and mimeographed his textbook on stage direction, directed operatic scenes with live singers, and conducted an orchestra. I had also managed a three-piano-and-orchestra tour of the United States and had cooked dinner all one summer for him, his mother, and some of the staff at the Tanglewood, Massachusetts, opera workshop. At approximately $1.25 an hour.

Of all the odd jobs I performed, conducting the orchestra was the most terrifying. Probably this is because I couldn't read an orchestral score, but the orchestra didn't know it.

But then, I brought it on myself. The summer I cooked for the Goldovskys at Tanglewood, did secretarial work, and took the stage directing course, I figured I would stay on with the gang and go to Mr. G.'s next summer assignment, a conducting workshop at Chatham College in Pittsburgh.

Mr. Goldovsky asked me to drive one of his cars from Tanglewood to Pittsburgh for his convenience. I shared the trip with a soprano named Annabelle Bernard. We had a wonderful time, talking and stopping to buy hot dogs and laughing. As we cruised along the Pennsylvania Turnpike, Annabelle was at the wheel and had a habit of driving in the left-hand passing lane. A brown car began to tailgate us, blowing the horn. I said to Annabelle, "You'd better move over to the right lane, he wants to pass."

The wind rushing through the car windows prevented her hearing me clearly. "What did you say?" she yelled.

"I said..." but before I could finish, the brown car's driver leaned irritably on his horn. I thought he was being rude and impatient. To show how I felt, I turned around, put my fingers in my ears, and waved my hands like antlers.

He turned on his siren. It was an unmarked police car, and he pulled us over to the side of the road. "You were operating the vehicle continuously in the passing lane of the turnpike," he told Annabelle furiously. "That's against the law."

"I'm sorry," she gasped, "I didn't realize it." "But your FRIEND here," he said, pointing to me. "Your friend here thinks it's funny. Your friend here turns around and makes faces at other drivers. Your friend here would stop at an accident and laugh at the victims."

"No sir, I wouldn't!" I protested.

"So why do you make nasty gestures to other drivers, huh?"

"I thought you were being impatient to blow the horn like that. If I had known you were a policeman, I wouldn't have done it."

This made him apoplectic. "Oh, yeah? You thought I was impatient, huh? Well, you and your friend can just follow me off the turnpike right to the judge."

We followed him to a small town justice of the peace who fined us $25. I paid $15 of it, since it had all been my fault. The judge said to Annabelle, "This serious crime will be on your record for the rest of your life." Tears began to roll down her cheeks.

"Don't put it on her record!" I cried. "It was my fault!"

"She was driving!" snarled the judge, banging his gavel. The highway patrolman grinned in satisfaction.

I wondered later if some of their severity was due to the fact that Annabelle was black and you didn't see too many integrated automobiles in those days, even in Pennsylvania. On the other hand, I DID make antler-faces, didn't I?

We got to Chatham College just in time to settle into the dormitory and find out the course schedules. The conductors' workshop was no small thing. Serious prospective conductors had signed up under Goldovsky's Leadership Training Program. He thought that any talented young person whose ultimate goal was to manage an opera company should be able to perform every single job in the house. He or she should, accordingly, emulate Mr. Goldovsky, who not only administered his New England Opera Company but also stage directed and conducted the operas, eliminating a need for additional talent searches. Sarah Caldwell, the renowned and redoubtable head of the Boston Opera, had for a while been one of his protegees, living up spectacularly to the one person-opera company concept.

To justify my presence at Chatham College, where there was a cafeteria so I didn't need to cook, Goldovsky asked me if I wanted to take the conducting course. What a question to ask an opera lover! OF COURSE I wanted to take it. I had been conducting along with the record player for years. I would pretend the sofa was the chorus and give it cues. I would point to the standing lamp as the tenor aria began. Now I would get to find out how it should really be done.

Peter Paul Fuchs was the teacher, and the talented students included persons who later went on to manage such opera companies as Washington and Tulsa, to assistant-conduct major orchestras, and to coach singers at the Metropolitan, Chicago and San Francisco operas. There, too, stood I, holding my little baton and grinning happily like one of the Three Stooges.

About halfway through the course Goldovsky said to me, "You know, it is not fair to the other students if you are simply an auditor. You must take the final exam along with them."

"Well, I'd be GLAD to!" I gushed. "What is it?"

"You will conduct the Pittsburgh Symphony."

My legs buckled. "What are you saying? I can't read the orchestral music."

"You will learn to read the orchestral music. I'll give you an easy piece for the concert—maybe something with only two singers."

"You mean I'm going to conduct SINGERS TOO?"

"Naturally!" snorted Goldovsky. "We are conducting opera, after all."

He assigned me a duet from *Don Giovanni* and I spent the next two weeks sitting up till three in the morning staring cross-eyed at the orchestral score. I decided that the isolated occasional black note at the bottom of the huge page must belong to the timpani because it seemed to be going boomp-boomp. The jumbled masses of sixteenth-notes higher up were probably violins, since there were so many of them.

The day of the dress rehearsal I stood in my little flowered sundress before the jaded musicians of the Pittsburgh Symphony Orchestra, who were being paid extra out of a trust fund to endure this ordeal. I gave them a downbeat, as Mr. Fuchs had taught us to do, and immediately they all buried their faces in their chests and never looked up at me again until the piece was over.

As for managing the piano-and-orchestra tour, I found out what one-night stands were all about. Poor musicians. My instructions were to find the cheapest hotels available in every city and to book fifty rooms. You haven't seen a cheap hotel until you've seen the ones I managed to grub out in Latrobe, Pennsylvania, and Keokuk, Iowa.

The soloists stayed in jazzier places and got invited to dinner. They were Mr. Goldovsky and his uncle and aunt, the Russian duo-pianist team Luboshutz and Nemenoff. Goldovsky conducted from the piano. As a conductor, he held to the theory that temperamental or dictatorial behavior was childish and did not improve the performance of an orchestra. Consequently he seemed to drift off into a smiling, semi-conscious reverie once the orchestra began to play, and though he continued to wave the baton, he didn't seem to want to disturb the players lest it interrupt the music.

While the playing usually sounded all right, if not fiery or inspiring the way it often did when bastards conducted, the demeanor of the orchestra suffered a little from his lack of involvement. We got a letter from one of the tour city chairmen later, complaining that the musicians were not according proper respect to the provincial audiences (true) and were in fact chewing gum and reading paperback books during the performance.

Goldovsky, unruffled, shrugged away the complaint and dictated a reply to the effect that he had not been aware of any such thing. I, however, had noticed it; but I was still too much in awe of my job with a famous person to tell him so. It was years before I developed the nerve to suggest to a boss that he might be wrong. What a shame I couldn't be a secretary now that I'm a grown-up.

We were on the road for a month and I loved it, which is probably why I don't mind now flying from city to city to give speeches and stay in hotels. It's light-years easier now because I have only myself to take care of. Being in charge of fifty musicians and responsible for their comfort was harrowing, but they were generally pleasant people and Uncle Pierre Luboshutz was funny enough to have been a stand-up comic in the Catskills along with Frank Gallagher, our double-bass player.

My mother also seemed to love the fact that I was touring the country glamorously, because I was doing things she would never have been allowed to do. I have a feeling my father hated it, but she wouldn't let him tell me so. As for my grandmother, her worst fears were realized when she got a phone call from her cousin, Aunt Georgeoulla, in Indianapolis. "My son went down and saw Hope at the hotel traveling around with all those low-class *musicanti*," she reported. "It's a shame she doesn't stay home with her family and look for a nice man so she can settle down, instead of disgracing us all this way."

The best disgrace was yet to come. I had yet to live in New York.

7
MOVING TO THE BIG HOUSE

By the time I had worked for Mr. Goldovsky for a year and a half, I had moved with my Cambridge roommates into a roomier but far less charming apartment. The new landlady, Mrs. Harrington, called us up and screamed curses if we coughed or moved a chair. But I had no plans to move away because I had met some nice Boston Greeks and was scheduled to be one's bridesmaid in June, 1958. Every Greek knows you might meet prospective bridegrooms at somebody else's wedding.

And then the phone rang in Mr. Goldovsky's office and it was Marguerite Wickersham, the director of the Metropolitan Opera's National Council and Central Opera Service. She knew Goldovsky well, as did everyone in opera, and she knew he knew everybody. "I'm getting married and leaving New York," she announced. "Can you find a replacement for me among your souvenirs?"

Goldovsky turned and glanced at me. I was whipping through a letter full of XXX's on the old non-electric typewriter. "Would you like to work at the Metropolitan?" he asked absently, glancing through some papers as he held the phone.

"Gee, I don't know. Well, yes."

"Marguerite," he said into the phone, "I may have someone for you. I'll call you back." He turned to me. "I don't know if you can qualify for this job. They want an office *manager*, you see, and here you have only been a secretary (read "slave"). But after all, my dear, you cannot work for $1.25 an hour forever, and I can't afford more than that. They would pay you a little better. Besides, it *is* the Metropolitan." His shrug indicated that this last did not particularly impress him.

But it impressed the devil out of me. The METROPOLITAN, for heaven's sake, the greatest opera house in the country, from which emanated the broadcasts that had mesmerized my young life for the past fifteen years.

I went to New York for the interview. Two extremely elegant and charming women, board members of the Met, interviewed me, because the National Council office was a development branch that dealt intimately with the world's best-heeled opera lovers.

These National Council officers, Mrs. Lewis Douglas and Mrs. John Barry Ryan, were both millionaires and close personal friends of Rudolf Bing. Naturally even they could see I wasn't experienced enough to run that big office.

But they liked me and were happy that I had gone to Vassar. And I could now type at least twenty words a minute. Most important of all, I had worked for Boris Goldovsky, which is what they mean when they say you have to have Job Experience before you can ever get a Job. They didn't know I XXX-ed out words, and I didn't mention it. I assumed they didn't need a cook, so I didn't mention this talent either.

Someone else was hired for office manager. But I was hired for extra staff person. And on June 1, 1958, instead of being a bridesmaid in my friend Zoe's wedding in Boston, I began to work for the Metropolitan Opera in New York.

The chief reason I had looked for work in Boston in the first place was that I was afraid to go to New York. There were friends I could live with in Boston, but at that time I didn't know anyone living in New York. By now, however, I knew one person. And she lived in the Metropolitan Opera building itself.

The old Met Studio building was big and dirty and murky and full of dark red, and it reminded me of phantoms and disfigured weirdos in the cellar and leaking pipes. My friend Maude lived there. She was a slightly eccentric, middle-aged woman who had taken Mr. Goldovsky's Leadership Training Course at Tanglewood the summer before. She was a singing teacher and coach of sorts and an aspiring singer herself, piping along in a quavery, hoarse soprano when she directed her few students in scenes. She always played the young ingenue lead in these scenes and her chief student, a twenty-two-year-old baritone from Queens, played the hero. Maude had a desperate crush on him.

Though Maude was about forty-seven, she wore girlish dresses with ballerina skirts and little black slippers and had her reddish hair in a long ponytail with all sorts of small bows and flowers around it. I liked Maude. For all her eccentricity, she was a kind and generous soul and a loyal friend. Years later I ran into the student on whom she had had the crush. He had treated her with reverence and respect and had followed her every whim and suggestion—including allowing her to cut his toenails—until, suddenly, he got a twenty-year-old girlfriend. Maude took offense and interfered in his love life by phoning him at awkward moments. They argued bitterly, and he stopped taking singing lessons. By then I had left New York and, later, I lost touch completely with Maude. I fear that she may have felt her future was ruined and drifted slowly into bag-ladydom.

Maude lived in a studio in the upper floors of the old Met and there was an empty room next to it. Somehow she got a key to the empty room and, without asking permission of any authority, suggested I stay there temporarily while apartment-hunting. The room was a narrow cubicle of institutional grubbiness, with a window so grimy even Superman could not have seen through it. We shared a tiny bathroom with rust-colored appliances, a thick layer of dust and occasional swimming roaches. Nobody had a kitchen.

I should have minded all this, but it was Bohemian and it was IN the Metropolitan. Maude had long since adjusted to the lack of a kitchen. She loved baked potatoes and looked forward to the nights that a big, flashy tourist restaurant a few blocks away on Times Square would have a baked-potato-your-way festival, at which time she would go over and spend her limited funds on three of them.

When later I got my own apartment and invited Maude for dinner, she had two favorite alternating menus: meat loaf, which she was afraid to order in a restaurant, and corn-on-the-cob and sliced tomatoes, nothing else, the second time. Maude had good, honest taste, I thought.

As much as I like to cook, I enjoyed the kitchen-less period in the old Met studios because it meant I could eat every meal out in one of the hundreds of cheap, good joints in the vicinity of 39th and Broadway. Nowhere were coffee better or rolls crustier than in the hole-in-the-wall eateries of Manhattan. A favorite breakfast and lunch place was the Governor Cafeteria on Broadway, across the street from the main entrance of the old Met. Most of the garment district employees ate there and the cuisine reflected their tastes. For breakfast I reveled in hot bagels with cream cheese and lox, bialys, and French toast made out of thick slices of corn bread, a morsel I had never tasted before and haven't since except when I make it.

Before long I thought they had taken me for an old garment district regular, but I never fooled the guys at the Governor for a minute. One day I ate for lunch, for the first time ever, chicken soup with matzoh balls. What a delicacy! Two days later I came in hankering for another bowl.

In my magnolia-belt manner, I simpered, "Kin ah have matzoh-ball soup, please?"

The man behind the counter put down his spatula and gave me a long, unsmiling look. "You want matzoh balls?"

"Yes sir."

"You LIKE matzoh balls?"

"Yes sir, ah really do."

He turned to the kitchen and yelled, "Hey, Herb! The shiksa wants matzoh balls!"

How, I ask you, could he tell I was a shiksa? With my dark hair and Greek face, I could perfectly well have been Jewish. Or at least a New Yorker. Was it something about the way I had....

Well, of course it was, but before long I could have had him fooled. Within a few months I no longer trembled and dropped my purse on the bus when the driver yelled at me for taking too long to get out my fare. "Wassa matter, sistah, ya wanna buy the bus? Take ya toime, get out ya life's savins, go wan."

By September I could look him in the eye and say, "What, buy DIS bus? You crazy? Dis bus is older'n yer mudder-in-lawr."

And he would smile at me affectionately and say, "Go ahead, siddown, ya can pay me when ya geddoff."

The National Council of the Metropolitan was essentially a fund-raising office and I hate fund-raising but, thank God, I was just a secretary and didn't have to do it. I typed and filed and figured I was the luckiest clerk in the arts because as an official employee of the Met I had my own key to a Secret Door that led from the dinky old studio building in which the National Council had its offices to the great opera auditorium itself. During my lunch hour, I could let myself into the house and watch a rehearsal. My first fall there, three of the greatest singers in the world were rehearsing *Tosca*.

It is hard to explain to a non opera-lover why a fan could hyperventilate sneaking into the huge, dark red and gold interior of the old Met, to sit somewhere near the stage and watch Renata Tebaldi, Mario del Monaco and Leonard Warren sing full voice and stop and laugh and joke with one another. A sports fan would probably have had the same reaction being able to sit down in the dugout with the famous players during the World Series.

It occurred to me recently that I never asked for anybody's autograph or picture in all the years I worked at the Metropolitan. Basically I don't like to ask celebrities for things like that; if, under general social pressure, I do, then I don't know what to do with the thing once I've got it and I lose it. Besides, I always felt I would get to see these famous people again tomorrow. Looking back now that a lot of the wonderful stars I knew on a first-name basis are either retired or dead or have amnesia, I wonder if it might not have been wonderful to have a personal missive or two from some of them to hand down to the next generation. But it's too late. If you are an opera lover, and even if you're not, you must trust me.

The first celebrities I actually met, working in an office dealing with contributions rather than artistic events, were tycoons.

I regret to say that I don't remember many of their names because it was far less acceptable for staff to fraternize with the wealthy patrons than with the stars they patronized. I do know we were supposed to be desperately careful not to do anything to offend them. Letters we wrote had to be perfect and protocol was a staggeringly big deal, lest a benefactor run tell Mr. Bing he was cutting off funds because of some flunky's gaucherie.

I made plenty of protocol mistakes later when working for Bing, having a goofy and inexcusable predilection for answering the phone in weird accents or forgetting to note extraordinarily important secretary-type things such as the date and hour of an important luncheon meeting. I was simply not a very good secretary by nature or skill. The only thing that had saved me with Goldovsky was his impatience with pretense and unnecessary paperwork, even if he did treat most people around him—and this included family as well as staff—with an amused, absentminded condescension.

But I was not yet aware that I might have to shape up enough secretarially to work for Rudolf Bing. That job was already taken and as out of reach to the likes of me as Jupiter. Me, be an executive secretary, and to a man by now famous for his impatience and temper?

I plowed through the tedious, ultra-polite correspondence in the National Council and enjoyed my little key to the Big House and moved into a small apartment which I could afford only because it was over a bar from which garbage smells wafted. My parents came to visit frequently, worrying a little that I lived alone but enjoying having a home base in New York, and I thought I was settled enough now in work to begin looking on the side for some unmarried Greeks or opera singers.

And then, practically on a silver platter, came the offer of the opportunity about which I had fantasized briefly at age fourteen. Bing's long-suffering secretary of some eight years had decided to everyone's astonishment to get married and then pregnant. This was the accepted order in those days. A little against her will she conceded that she would have to leave the ideal opera-lover's job.

A memo was circulated throughout the organization. Did any in-house secretary wish to apply for this prestigious position? Bing had a phobia of hiring and of employment agencies and wanted someone who already knew the difference between the Metropolitan Opera and soap opera, not that there really is that much difference.

Somebody in the National Council office said, "Why don't you go down for the interview? You always wanted to meet singers up close."

"Are you kidding? I can't even take shorthand."

"So what? Bing doesn't know that."

Yes, why reveal something like this to a prospective employer? Shorthand was really no problem, because I took the subway to work every day and there was a big green ad over the seats for a speedwriting school. I stared at it every morning. It said:

"f y k rd ths msj y 2 k bkm a stno & ern hi pa."

I thought, "f i k rd tht msj, I don't need to go to their dumb school."

I went down to Bing's office for the interview. I had to traverse a long, noisy hallway with a linoleum floor, go past a couple of hot plates and an ancient sofa, and present myself at a narrow cubicle occupied by two secretaries—one Bing's, the other his assistant John Gutman's. Reva was Bing's secretary, and I was afraid of her then. Later we became friends and shared a certain bittersweet amusement as veterans of a difficult job. I had the feeling that day that she didn't want to leave at all but was being forced out by the administration because they were afraid of pregnant women.

Bing buzzed for me to come in. I went down a little step into his homey-looking, carpeted, old-fashioned office, with its minuscule bathroom about a foot away from the desk, and a sofa and chair for famous singers to perch on. On a coffee table was his favorite photo of himself arm-in-arm with Maria Callas.

Bing was tall and thin, with fine, slightly hawkish features and thinning hair. He was dressed in perfectly-tailored British clothes and had an aristocratic air. He took one look at me and said, "Ach, Gott, it will never work."

I wondered if I had B.O. or looked too Greek.

He repeated, with an irritable tsk, "It will never work. You are much too young." Then he heaved a heavy sigh and added, "But what can I do? No one else is applying for the job. Gott. Sit down and take a letter."

I knew better than to mention shorthand. I picked up the pad and pencil. Bing began, "Dear Graf."

Ye gods, he was dictating a letter to the famous stage director Herbert Graf. It was about operas and foreign houses and things I could spell, though, and Bing dictated at a dramatic, rhetorical pace that made it easy to keep up. When he was finished, he fixed me with a steely, authoritarian eye and commanded in his Viennese accent, "Go now to your office and type this letter. If you discover something in your notes that you cannot understand, DO NOT try to guess what it is. Come at once to find me, no matter what I am doing, and ask me what I dictated. I will not have inaccuracies and fabrications leaving this office. Do you understand?"

"Yes sir." I was frozen with terror.

As I left his office to slink back up through the dark passageways to my little desk, I could hear him muttering, "Ach, Gott, it will never work."

His warning had been well-taken. I got to a sentence in my notes that appeared to say "You are an internal stage director." Now, that was peculiar. Internal? Well, I could always find ways to justify things. Maybe what Bing had meant to say was "introspective." Someone who looks into his Inner Soul for inspiration in stage directing, that's what he meant to convey. I typed "internal" nonetheless, made sure there were no smudges or erasures—and, God knows, no XXX's—and brought the finished letter down for him to read.

He skimmed through it rapidly, scowling, and then stopped, pounded his fist on the desk and turned red. "Here it is! You see? You have done EXACTLY what I warned you not to do. I knew this would never work. It is not 'internal' stage director that I have said! How can it be inTERnal? What in Gott's name does this mean? I said 'interNATIONAL!' You have failed your first test in this interview."

I looked blindly about the room for a weapon with which to commit suicide. "But," Bing added, "what can I do? Nobody else has applied for this job. And you have, of course, worked for Goldovsky. This is not the greatest endorsement in the world but at least you are familiar with the milieu. Ach, GOTT! Report on Monday."

And with this warm and generous welcome ringing in my ears, I went back up to the National Council to tell the other secretaries I had gotten the job and then went home to tremble and worry. Fortunately, my mother was visiting from Virginia.

I told Mama, then my only confidante, that I had been offered a plum job but was afraid to take it. We agonized about it all evening. Finally, she said, "It's a wonderful job and you're smart and quick and the best person he could ever get." She was my mother, after all. "I say go on and take the job. And if he doesn't like the way you do the work and talks mean to you, just tell him to go to hell and come home."

8

FROM OPERA TO UPROAR

The first day I worked on my own as Rudolf Bing's secretary, with no Reva sitting next to me unsmiling, saying, "Don't think there's any glory in this job," I had the treat I had been looking forward to as an opera lover. My desk calendar read, "Del Monaco, 11 A.M."

My heart pounded wildly because Mario Del Monaco was one of the greatest Italian tenors in the world and I had never seen him up close before. It was early March and cold, with snow flurries. At one minute to eleven, Del Monaco and his wife came lumbering down the hall wearing ankle-length mink coats. I thought briefly of grizzly bears and said in a voice gushing with hospitality, "I'll tell Mr. Bing that you're here. Please make yourselves comfortable."

I buzzed Bing and reported the arrival of the mink coats and he said irritably, "Yes, tell them to wait. Get me Kurt Herbert Adler on the telephone."

As I placed the call to the San Francisco Opera, I wondered why Mrs. Del Monaco had come in with her husband. Later I discovered that nearly every great Italian tenor brought a woman along with him for the negotiation of his contract. Del Monaco and Corelli brought their wives. Eugenio Fernandi came in with his mother. During these negotiations, the women usually spoke more than the men, who were apparently saving their voices and were well aware that the Met management was afraid of Italian women.

After seven minutes, Del Monaco got up from the couch and walked over to my tiny roll-top desk to nod and smile. I took his meaning and buzzed Bing a second time. "Did I mention that the Del Monacos are here, sir?"

"Yes, of course you told me. They will have to wait. Bring me the Kirsten file."

I tried to make a little small talk with Mr. Del Monaco but he stared at the ceiling and whistled tunelessly. Mrs. Del Monaco sat with her eyes closed. Eight minutes elapsed. Del Monaco leaned perilously close to me over the desk top. "Mr. Bing perhaps does not understand what you tell him?"

"I'm sure it's just some emergency, sir!" I was hoarse by now with fear. I buzzed Bing.

"I hope," he hissed, "that you are not going to tell me Del Monaco is here. I am well aware of this incredible nuisance. Offer him some coffee." This was a peculiar suggestion since we did not have a coffee pot. I declined the advice, smiled blazingly at the Del Monacos and started to type a list of sample resignation notices.

After five minutes Bing buzzed me on the intercom. I picked up the phone and he said, "Wheel Del Monaco in." In the little flush of pleasure I felt at the fact that the big boss was sharing humor with me, I walked right past the couch on which the Del Monacos had been sitting and then realized that they weren't there.

I ran out to the reception desk at the stage door. "Where are the Del Monacos?"

"They got tired of waiting," said Winnie the receptionist. "They went for a walk."

Without coat or hat I ran out into the snow flurries. A block and a half away, the grizzly bears lumbered along. I caught up with them. "Mr. Bing will see you now!"

"Bing makes-a me wait, I make-a heem wait," declared Del Monaco.

They took eight minutes to walk back. Bing buzzed me hysterically the whole time. When at last they stood outside his door and he threw it open to welcome them, I expected a vicious rending of flesh and perchance a grenade from Mrs. Del Monaco's purse. Instead, Bing opened his arms wide and cried, "Del Monaco!"

"Mr. Bing!" cried Del Monaco in a voice rich with affection and emotion.

They hugged, went in and signed a contract immediately. Opera negotiations, I realized then, are beyond the scope of sales trainers and management consultants. They are more properly the province of crystal-ball readers and the sort of crazy relatives from whom you fear the kids will inherit genes.

In the months that followed, awed acquaintances with great singers grew into fond friendships. Terror of administrators and conductors mellowed into awed acquaintance.

While I never overcame my basic fear of Rudolf Bing, I soon became enormously fond of two of his assistant managers, John Gutman and Francis Robinson. Mr. Gutman was witty and affectionate, a courtly European. Mr. Robinson, though less approachable, was a charming Southern gentleman, the perfect public relations man and a favorite of artists and wealthy patrons.

There were also Herman Krawitz, a tough boss of the old school, yelling like a prison warden at the secretaries, Robert Herman, a hearty, hideously well-organized man with a pretend smile who hadn't noticed yet that the secretaries weren't robots, and Paul Jaretzki, a kind, shy man who knew that they were human beings.

And there were all the other secretaries—intelligent, witty, mostly unmarried, long-suffering opera lovers. I shared the cubicle with Bob Herman's secretary, Florence Guarino, a suave, petite, extremely charming woman in her late thirties. She had been there longer than any of the male administrators and could have run the place but wouldn't have dreamed of doing it. She was a nurturing secretary of the old school with one major difference: the men were afraid of her and would have been doomed without her. And she knew it. In addition, there were the two witty and intelligent women who were secretaries to Gutman and Jaretzki, Louise Florian and Anne Cotton. They were first-rate friends and comrades and fun to be around.

Winnie Short and Mary Colligan presided over the reception desk and they were probably my favorite people at the

Metropolitan Opera. Both of them were down-to-earth Irish women with New York accents and, for all their seeming lack of elegant operatic mannerisms, more knowledgeable about the world's singers and their habits than any fifty managers put together.

Once, for example, someone asked me to get Leontyne Price on the telephone. I buzzed Mary at the switchboard to ask if she knew how to reach Miss Price. Mary, in a voice not unlike Edith Bunker's, asked Winnie, "Where's Leontyne this month?"

"She's at the Rome Opera."

"Let's see," said Mary, "It's around six o'clock there now, right Winnie? You think she's gone to supper yet?"

"No, I bet she's resting at her *pensione*. The guy who runs that place is called Umberto, remember? Put in the call and I'll talk to him, he knows my voice by now. And if she's not there, she's probably over at that little coffee place across the street. I've got the number right here."

Within ten minutes they would have Leontyne Price on the phone, reached at her cappuccino cup halfway around the world.

The first week I was there I also learned about priorities. Not being by nature or experience a true secretary, I didn't know the essentials about Keeping The Boss Happy and they would never have occurred to me. Bing buzzed me at four P.M. and said "Please bring me my tea now."

Reva had told me about tea. Even though Bing was an Austrian, he was a British citizen and relished every minute of it, from bowler and umbrella to tea at four o'clock, except that he revealed his true background by taking the tea with lemon and six cubes of sugar.

In the old Metropolitan building, electric current had not yet caught up with the mid-twentieth century. There was one outlet in the office that could handle the voltage of the electric hot water pot, and my typewriter was plugged into it. At that moment, I was retyping Tebaldi's contract and her agent was waiting for it. Obviously the tea had to wait.

In five minutes, Bing buzzed me again. "Where is my tea?"

"Sir, as soon as I finish typing the Tebaldi contract I can plug in the teapot."

He sighed. "There are plenty of other sopranos in the world. Bring me my tea."

The priorities had been established. I made the tea and took it in, and he reached into his briefcase and took out a little waxed-paper sandwich bag containing half a sandwich of German sausage on rye bread with butter. "Please put this on a plate so that I can have it with my tea."

When I brought the sandwich in, he snapped, "Where is the waxed-paper bag?"

"I threw it away."

"I am not a millionaire. I will tell you when to throw away the bag. Please get it at once."

I went out and rummaged through the trash until I found the balled-up paper bag. He smoothed it out, folded it, and put it back in his briefcase, and it stayed in use for another two months. Now I understood why the Met ran in the black during his tenure.

But I really wasn't happy doing the nurturing secretary things. I had always thought wives did those things, such as write thank-you notes for dinner parties, take men's suits to the cleaners, get items mended or repaired. To my surprise I found that Mrs. Bing never did any of these things, never had and never would. I never knew what Mrs. Bing did at all, except come on rare occasion to the opera house to sit in the general manager's box when there were important guests. Even though I was introduced to her two or three times in those four years I worked there, I know she never knew who or what I was. To tell you the truth, I'm not sure Mr. Bing really knew who I was either. I thought he just couldn't pronounce my last name, but in retrospect I would say he never knew what it was.

And so it fell on the staff to take care of Mr. Bing's needs and some of them were sharp enough to take this far more seriously than I did. One day Mr. Bing handed me his ubiquitous

New Year's Eve at the Met, 1961. Rudolf Bing in a good mood with grinning secretary Hope.

black umbrella and said, "Ach, Gott, this doesn't work properly any more. Would you please have it repaired?"

The yellow pages revealed that there was an umbrella repair shop a few blocks away off Broadway. I took it there at lunch hour and the man gave me a ticket and said it would take about ten days because there were a lot of repairs ahead of me.

When I told this to Bing he was distressed. "Gott, ten days! What will I do without it? Well, I suppose it can't be helped."

Half an hour later, a young administrative assistant named Henry appeared, tossed his head back, straightened his impeccably-tailored shoulders and tapped his fingers nervously on my desk. "Give me the ticket for Mr. Bing's umbrella repair," he ordered. I gave it to him, even though he was an underling too. I hadn't been there long enough to ask questions.

Two hours later, Henry dashed in holding Mr. Bing's umbrella, totally repaired. "I'll take this in to him," he snorted.

To Bing's credit, he could see through this sort of chicanery even if he did appreciate it. "Well, well!" he told me with a sardonic smile. "Henry has gotten my umbrella repaired in a few hours even though you told me it would take ten days. How remarkable!"

"How wonderful!" I cried, thinking The Sonofabitch.

The part I had looked forward to most at the opera house, meeting the singers, more than made up for anything mundane or clerical I had to do. How can people work in a place they don't like? I wondered sometimes, while filing lists or typing the same things over and over or making phone calls I really didn't like to make. As long as the lists and letters and calls were about opera, I was happy.

The singer I liked most to see was Jon Vickers, the Canadian tenor. Like many of the women who worked in the house, I had a fierce crush on him because he was attractive, very masculine, a wonderful singing actor and—whether we realized or not that this was a reason for his charm—a fabulous husband and father. A glance or hug from Jon Vickers could give one of us pleasant dreams for the next five years. One time, elated by an ovation after one of his arias, he came backstage radiant and grinning, saw me standing in the wings like a lovesick teenaged fan, grabbed me in his arms and ran up a short flight of stairs holding me.

Twenty-five years later I came to the Metropolitan one evening with my mother and my nineteen-year-old daughter. We saw Jon Vickers in *Pagliacci* and went backstage afterwards to meet him. We stood at the end of a long line of opera fans, all of whom talked importantly about times he had signed autographs for them before and things they had written him. He spotted me and gave me the same dazzling smile he had given me when I was a star-struck secretary, and when we finally got to him he embraced me like a long-lost family member and we reminisced. My daughter relished more than anything the faces of the other fans. "He really DID care about us!" she observed—which is probably what it was about Jon Vickers that made us love him.

Another tenor on whom I had a crush was Nicolai Gedda, the wonderful Swedish-Russian artist who had perfect diction in every language and enormous courtly charm in every situation. Even better, he was a bachelor. When my roommates and

I had parties, I sometimes invited him and other opera singers and he always amazed and delighted us by attending. After one party, some of the people stayed late, and Nicolai Gedda sat with me at the piano and sang like a pop singer. Then he and another tenor, Gabor Carelli, did a scene from *La Boheme* with Carelli singing the soprano part. But my greatest claim to fame is the Date I had with Nicolai Gedda. He stopped by my desk one afternoon and asked if I had seen "Never on Sunday," the movie that was the big rage those days in New York. It was the first Greek movie of note that had ever come to the USA. Gedda asked me to go with him since I might be able to translate parts that the sub-titles missed. I was frantic with excitement.

We went to the movie and then walked back to the apartment I shared with two college friends, and all the way up Madison Avenue Gedda did Greek dances and sang the "Never on Sunday" theme song. Then he came in and had coffee and food with us and charmed my roommates.

Like about a thousand other women I wanted to marry Nicolai Gedda, but I didn't know how to work it out. A tough and aggressive press agent named Marianna also wanted him, and she convinced me to have a little party and invite both her and him and a handful of other people she wanted to get to know. Will you please tell me why I did this? When Gedda walked in and saw her, he paled and spent the rest of the evening falling over furniture trying to get away from her. He probably figured I'd do it again and avoided me from that day forward. As it turned out, I married a Russian and Gedda later married a Greek-American—so we both more or less stuck to my original plan.

If I had really wanted romance, I could have had it with absolutely no problem by encouraging Eugenio Fernandi. This poor guy was a perfectly good tenor who had rather a large cross to bear—his six-foot-two, 300-pound mother. For that matter, Eugenio was built the same way, and they made a formidable pair lumbering down the narrow hallway towards Mr. Bing's office. The one difference between mother and son was attitude.

Eugenio was good-natured, obsequious and cheerful; his mother was grim, steely-eyed and suspicious. She handled his career.

The Met management learned early on that 1) they had to deal with Mama Fernandi, and 2) she wasn't easy to deal with. Like many of the strong Italian women who took charge of their men's singing careers, Mama F. knew the value both of stony silence and thunderous argument. Even when the Met managers thought they had won, Mama would generally come out triumphant.

A perfect example is of the occasion, during my first few months in the general manager's office, on which the Met had a problem on tour casting the tenor in *La Traviata*. The Metropolitan used to go on a lengthy tour after its New York season, bringing live opera in those more deprived days to cities such as Atlanta, Boston, Minneapolis, Memphis, and Dallas. They traveled both by train and plane, and it was murder packing hundreds of employees—singers, administrators and immense production staff—and their luggage into a couple of trains and planes, to say nothing of the huge pieces of scenery. I can't remember whether the latter would even fit into railroad cars or whether they had to be transported on grueling, all-night truck drives.

The Met had just arrived in Boston, and I sat happily at my desk in New York, relieved temporarily of the terror of Mr. Bing's buzz. Suddenly Robert Herman, Bing's no-nonsense assistant, was on the phone from Boston with unusual instructions. "Stop whatever you're doing and go to the train station and buy two tickets for the one o'clock train to Boston. Then go to Eugenio Fernandi's hotel, pick up Fernandi and his mother and escort them to the station, and MAKE SURE they get on the train. We've scheduled him for *Traviata* tonight but he doesn't want to sing it."

I bought two tickets for the Yankee Clipper and headed for the hotel on the upper West Side where the Fernandis made their home while in New York. My Italian at that point was severely limited and the Fernandis spoke no English. I called their room and yelled—remember, you always raise your voice in another language—"SON QUI. HO I BIGLIETTI." This meant, I think, "I'm here and I've got the tickets."

Fernandi bubbled effusively that they would be right down. Ten minutes went by and they weren't. I telephoned their room again. This time it was Mama Fernandi, considerably less pleasant. They had a lot of packing to do, she said, and they were almost ready. My wristwatch read 12:35 P.M.

At 12:44, just as I was picking up the house phone again with a sweaty palm, the elevator doors opened and the Fernandis emerged, two giant six-footers, one of them gray haired and angry, the other red-faced under slick, black hair, smiling apologetically. They were carrying, for their two-day stay in Boston, three large suitcases and assorted bags full of jars of tomato sauce, salamis, cheeses, and loaves of bread, opera scores and Italian newspapers.

Fernandi cashed a couple of travelers' checks and I ran out to the hotel entrance to get a cab. It was 12:50. No driver in his right mind wanted to stop for giants with baggage and a hysterical female jumping in and around the bags like a grasshopper. I threw open a cab door before the driver could slap on his Off Duty sign and we took off with screeching tires for the train station, I urging the driver on as though I were a stagecoach driver, the Fernandis reverting to type. I was wedged between them in the back seat, and Mama Fernandi spent the ride directing toward my right ear, from a distance of one inch, a diatribe against the management of the Metropolitan, its insensitivity to her son's artistic preferences, and the inadequacy of its costume department which routinely, she barked, made his trousers too tight in the crotch. She attempted to illustrate this last by leaning over me to point at the region in question on Fernandi.

He, hapless man, stared silent and blushing out of the taxi window, pinching me surreptitiously from time to time. As we pulled up to the train station, its huge outdoor clock read 1:00 P.M. Trains wait for no one, no one. Bob Herman had said to me, his tone heavy with foreboding, "No matter what else you do today, make SURE the Fernandis catch that train."

I leaned over Fernandi (he liked that), flung open the door, pushed him and fell out with him, then ran like a madwoman into the terminal, scattering people viciously right and left, until I spotted a conductor. Flinging myself at him, I grabbed him by both arms and shouted, "Don't let the Yankee Clipper leave for Boston! I've got an Italian tenor here who has to get there to sing in *La Traviata* and his mother weighs 300 pounds!"

Something unusual in my aspect penetrated the customary reserve of the railroad employee. Rushing towards a nearby gate, he roared, "STOP THE YANKEE CLIPPER!" And from the bowels of the station we heard the mournful shrieks of a train grinding to a stop. The Fernandis, dropping salamis in their wake, boarded, and I sprinted back to the Met, fell behind my desk and called the corner sandwich shop to order a double Regular Coffee, which means lots of cream and sugar, and a chopped-liver sandwich on pumpernickel, which I deserved. My job was secure.

Next morning Mr. Herman made his usual routine call. "Did Fernandi get there all right?" I asked. "How did he sing?"

"He didn't," said Mr. Herman. "His mother said he had a sore throat, so he canceled."

But this was not my last encounter with the bumbling, kind-hearted Fernandi, who somehow resembled a giant panda and whose mother, we had heard, clipped his toenails and still scrubbed his back when he bathed. He stopped me one day in a hall at the opera house and, glancing in terror over his shoulder, asked me to meet him after work at Bill's Bar, the Met staff's favorite watering-place on West 40th Street. In Italian, he beseeched me to keep this meeting a secret. Don't worry, I thought, I'm afraid of your mother too.

At Bill's he had an orange juice and I a beer, and we tried with amiable grins to overcome the language barrier. Every few minutes he would reach across the little table to clutch my hands and, shaking his head deliriously and looking heavenward, would cry, "Ah, sono tanto felice!" He was so happy, he said, and it was word for word from a couple of opera librettos I knew.

The last time I saw Eugenio socially, before his return to Italy at the end of his contract, was at one of those tiny gatherings my roommates and I threw from time to time in our one-room apartment—a cocktail party for some 250 people. I invited Fernandi but couldn't think how to explain in Italian that it was relatively casual and just a big open house.

Mistaking the invitation for something a bit more intimate, he arrived in black tie, holding a bouquet of red roses and his latest recording of Puccini's *Turandot* with Maria Callas. I was delighted but guilty, because I never said more than two more words to him that evening, as he got shoved and pushed from group to group by all the young stockbrokers and secretarial assistants my roommates had invited. People smoked in those days and the air was bad for singers, so Fernandi apologized profusely and left.

Bless his poor heart, he never returned to the Met. Some opera manager demanded that his mother not accompany him to every rehearsal and meeting, thinking it would make him stronger and more independent. Instead it made him distraught and insecure and, in time, undermined his vocal ability—or so we amateur psychiatrists determined, hearing that he was no longer singing in major houses.

Our chief regret in losing the Fernandis at the Met was losing Mama F.'s Christmas presents of homemade ravioli or pizza. She only gave these to the managers but Bing hated Italian food and routinely shoved the package over to me, muttering, "Ach, Gott. Write Mrs. Fernandi and thank her for the wonderful pizza again. Gott."

Temperament and intrigue were not confined to the male singers. Maria Callas, of course, took the Temperament Prize, but—alas—she had been fired by Bing for insubordination a few months before I came to work in his office. This meant I would not get to see the great soprano, arguably the best operatic actress who ever lived, performing live on stage.

I was certainly not the only one irritated by this circumstance. The Maria Callas fan club raised hell, picketing the house, making threatening phone calls, writing obscene letters to the management. Bing wasn't frightened by these things but he was clearly alarmed by the possibility of some sort of demonstration taking place on the night that Mme. Callas' replacement made her debut. The new soprano was Leonie Rysanek, a distinguished Austrian singing actress known to be easily offended by unruly critics and audiences. Rysanek would make her Met debut as Lady Macbeth in Verdi's *Macbeth*, the role Callas would have sung, and there was general terror that the Callas fans would fill standing room that night and boo or disrupt. Extra security guards were hired; signs were posted warning standees of dire consequences should they misbehave.

We all dressed up and came to the performance that night, in a state of great unease. There were pickets outside the house and a feeling of tension everywhere. Lady Macbeth makes her entrance holding a letter, which she reads aloud before beginning to sing. Rysanek strode down to the edge of the stage, unfurled the letter and began to read in a clear, loud voice. Suddenly, up in the Family Circle standing room, somebody yelled, "BRAVO, CALLAS!"

A frisson of terror went through the house. Here comes the riot, we thought. And then the conductor, Erich Leinsdorf, brought down his baton and began the introductory music to Lacy Macbeth's aria. As though she had heard nothing from the Family Circle, Rysanek began to sing. We will never know whether or not Callas would have done it better. But when Rysanek was finished, there was a standing ovation—as much for her courage under stress as for her singing ability.

It was not until several years later, when Rudolf Bing wrote his first book of memoirs, *5000 Nights at the Opera* , that I found out what had happened that night. Unbeknownst even to me, his secretary, he had telephoned the head of the Maria Callas fan club and offered him money, payable by check from an usher when he got to the opera house, to shout "Brava, Callas!" once Mme. Rysanek made her appearance. Bing said he knew Americans loved an underdog and that they would give Rysanek a warm reception if they felt she were being harassed. An astonishing risk that paid off!

One thing that was fun about famous singers is that often they were charmingly down to earth in their habits. An example was the wonderful American soprano Eileen Farrell. She was married to a policeman with a pronounced New York accent, and the two of them brightened everyone's day when they entered the Met. Eileen's husband liked to pal around near the switchboard, where he found instant soulmates in Mary and Winnie.

Sometimes when Eileen was singing some spectacular and powerful role up on the stage, he would stick his head around the corner and call, "Hey, Winnie, stop talkin' so much. Yer creatin' a draft and it might give Eileen a sore throat."

Eileen herself, the day of her first rehearsal at the Met, was accompanied to the rehearsal room by Merle Hubbard, a young rehearsal assistant and devoted opera fan. Later Merle reported that Miss Farrell, in hitting a spectacular high note, grabbed at her pearl necklace and it broke and scattered pearls all over the floor. Immediately, he and several others fell to their knees to pick up the pearls.

"Ah, forget it, kids," belted Farrell. "It's only a buck ninety-eight."

Another diva who occasionally acted out of character was Zinka Milanov. Dressed in her jewels and mink stole, she would go over to the Burger Pit in the next block, sit at the counter and call out in her stentorian Slavic accent, "Geeve me Swiss chiz on rye, planty of mustard."

One of the stage managers, Stanley Levine, escorted Milanov down to the dark and leaky basement under the stage one evening so that she could make her entrance from there up onto the supposed rooftop in the last act of *Tosca*. She perched on a stool, pulling her long skirts up around her, and looked around at the leaking pipes and occasional skittering mice which caught the beam of Levine's flashlight.

"Vot's de matter, Levine?" she murmured. "Dey sent all the light bulbs to Lincoln Center already?"

Which brings to mind the enormous and rather traumatic differences between the old Metropolitan Opera House at 39th and Broadway and the new one at Lincoln Center Plaza, where the opera company moved in 1966. What was traumatic was the change in ambience, a change many of us still feel was for the worse.

The old Met may have had primitive working conditions, but it also had charm. The old place probably could have been renovated in certain ways—new plumbing and electricity, for instance—at far less cost than the jazzy new house. There was, however, really no way to organize the stage scenery without building a new place. The old Met had absolutely no storage space for scenery. Every time the Met put on an opera, which was every day and twice on Saturdays, trucks had to bring the huge stage sets from a warehouse up in the Bronx and stack them outdoors on the sidewalk against the building. If it rained, bad news. The wretched stagehands had to run out and cover them with tarps.

But, then, the stagehands were used to this. And the lack of good plumbing—only two toilets and one sink in the orchestra-level ladies' room, for example—had been borne cheerfully by patrons for over eighty years. Nobody minded the bad facilities because the theater was beautiful. It was ornate and had gilt trimmings on the boxes and red plush accessories and the wonderful proscenium arch with its huge gold curtain. It was The Met, and the acoustics were absolutely perfect.

When the new Met was built, most of the greatest grief came from attempts trying to achieve decent acoustics. Acoustical engineers were called in from all over the world, tests were made, construction was constantly altered. And do you know what? Acoustics were nowhere near as good as those in the old place, which had been built simply to give the richest patrons the best view with no thought whatever to the way things might sound up in the cheap balcony.

As for the executive offices, gone was the old camaraderie of the tiny, disorganized back wing of the old Met, with its grubby little rooms opening off a long, linoleum-floored hall. No longer might a secretary jump up from her old-fashioned, peeling desk and pop into the room next door to comment on something she had just heard through the wall. Now people had to make long walks down carpeted corridors to other wings, and since there was never time to do this, employees generally just buzzed each other instead and lost personal contact.

Perhaps it is simply nostalgia, but those of us who saw opera in the old place still think singers sounded better there. And they probably did, because of the acoustics and the smaller size of the house, a grateful size for unamplified singing. And, by the same token, we seem to have seen more interesting things on the stage there.

There was the night Jan Peerce, singing in *Lucia di Lammermoor*, seemed to be chewing gum during the first act. At one point, observers in the employees' box swore they had seen him blow a bubble. "How," someone asked, "will he negotiate that bubble gum when he sings the aria in a minute?"

It was no problem. With a dramatic gesture, Peerce struck his hand meaningfully against his mouth and then slapped it against a piece of scenery. He had pulled out the gum and stuck it onto a safe place for later retrieval.

But the best events took place on tour, out of sight of the demanding and critical New York subscribers. By now legendary is the night in Boston that Birgit Nilsson, the great Swedish soprano, held a note longer than Franco Corelli, who had near apoplexy about it later in the dressing room. He threatened to quit that instant until Bing cleverly suggested he bite Nilsson in the next act. Apparently he lost his nerve, but later Nilsson sent Bing a telegram from Minneapolis, the next stop on the tour. "Corelli bit me tonight," she wired, "am being treated for rabies."

A baritone of my acquaintance related a charming incident in which he was involved in a small provincial opera house in Italy. He was singing *Rigoletto*, which meant he had to be a hunchback. The costume department had fitted him out appropriately in an outfit that had a huge hump sewn into it. In the middle of a tender duet with his daughter Gilda, he felt the hump loosen itself from its moorings and slide inexorably downward until it became a mammoth rear end which he had to drag around the stage behind him until the end of the act.

Sometimes you wonder which stories are true and which apocryphal, but I know a lot of people who will swear to having witnessed a production of *Tosca* somewhere in the Midwest, during which the soprano, who jumps to her death from a tall building, somehow irritated the stagehands. Instead of putting mattresses behind the set for her to land on, they put a trampoline, and the old gal came up six times after her suicide.

The one dramatic occasion, however, which I attended personally and can remember in detail was one that was in no way amusing. It will stay in my memory all my life. Renata Tebaldi, one of the most revered of Italian sopranos, was singing in Verdi's *La Forza Del Destino* for the first time that season in March 1960. The all-star cast included other distinguished singers: Richard Tucker, Cesare Siepi, and probably one of the greatest baritones who ever lived, Leonard Warren.

We secretaries took turns having night duty during the season. There was always the possibility that emergency paperwork might come up during a performance. I was on duty that night, and instead of going out to sit in the employees' box near the stage, I sat back in the office at my desk typing some letters. I could hear the performance in progress from the little loudspeaker over the door.

Suddenly I heard silence. It was a lengthy silence, longer than the usual pause between scenes, and there were muffled voices and coughs in the background. Just as I was standing to go out to the stage for a look, members of the artistic staff came running down the corridor and into the office next to mine. I heard Bob

Herman calling to Mary at the switchboard as he entered his office, "Get me Mario Sereni on the phone right away!"

They need a replacement, I thought. I wonder why? And then there was Bob Herman's voice, through the wall, shaky with emotion, saying to Sereni in Italian, "Come here immediately. Mr. Warren is very sick."

Leonard Warren sick? I had just heard him in good voice a few minutes ago over the loudspeaker. I went to the stage. The wings were packed with people—choristers, technicians, stage management. The stage lights were on and there was an eerie silence. A stage manager next to me murmured, "Warren collapsed. It doesn't look good."

In a matter of moments, the tenor Richard Tucker, a longtime personal friend of Warren, came into the wings from the stage, sobbing. Mrs. Warren, who had been watching the performance from a box with her family priest, stood to the side shaking her head in a daze. The house doctor, Adrian Zorgniotti, came wearily into the wings, having tried in vain for some twenty minutes to resuscitate the great baritone, who had pitched forward, dead of a cerebral hemorrhage, in the middle of an aria after the words, "Oh, joy! Joy!"

The audience, a packed house, had been told that Mr. Warren was sick. They sat quietly, waiting for an announcement about a possible replacement. Bing prepared to go out to make the dread announcement, and those of us who were on duty that night went to the employees' box to hear him. His words remain clearly in my memory: "Ladies and gentlemen, Leonard Warren, one of the greatest baritones who has ever sung at the Metropolitan, has just died." A gasp went through the house. "But he has died as every great performer would wish to die— at the height of his career, in the midst of one of his finest performances. I hope you will agree with me that, under these circumstances, we cannot continue with tonight's performance. Thank you."

In silence, except for occasional sobs and murmurs of shock, the hundreds of opera lovers filed out.

9
837 MADISON AVENUE

Though the job was glamorous, the best part of living in New York was, of course, living in New York. Young people who live there nowadays insist it's just as much fun and no scarier than it was in the early '60s. I won't argue with that, simply because I know how much I loved it in my post-college days and how others even then assumed it would be dangerous and dirty and frightening.

From my lone apartment on West 57th Street, the scary one above the bar, I moved—to my family's relief—to a huge, poorly-constructed newer building in the east '70s, preferable only because there were four other girls living there, acquaintances from Vassar. I loved the arrangement, despite the combat conditions in bedroom and bathroom, because the girls were fun and had interesting social lives and I envied this last—though in years to come they told me they had envied my unusual social life in the arts.

A dear friend and favorite person was Ann Grandy. She was from Virginia Beach and had also gone both to Turnbull's and Vassar. She had a remarkable sense of humor and an ear for mimicry. It was from Ann that I learned and perfected certain accent imitations that I use to this day in public speaking, in particular every possible type of Virginian Southerner. Ann and I would sit in public places talking to one another like Virginia teenagers: "Who do you date, Hope?" "Bubba Gwaltney. Who do you date?" "Girl, you do NOT date him! Ah KNOW who dates him."

Or pained Virginia aristocrats, looking concerned as they asked you, "Dawlin', how's your mummah? You tell her to come see me now, heah?"

Another roommate and close friend was Marlyn Mangus, a young woman of wit and great intelligence from Goodland, Kansas. Later the three of us moved into a different apartment at 837 Madison Avenue, a wonderfully attractive place with high ceilings and a fireplace but only one bedroom, and that the size of a pick-up truck. But the address was chic.

We had good parties there. And our decor, determined by things Ann's mother had sent from Virginia or that Marlyn, with her innate good taste, had bought on sale, was supplemented whimsically by oddities Marlyn brought home from work. She was a geologist on the staff of the American Museum of Natural History. Whenever the museum dismantled an exhibit and put things aside for the trash, Marlyn, ever thrifty and on the lookout for the unique, would comb through the rejects looking for things to bring home.

One day she came home with a stuffed penguin. It was near Eastertime, so we dyed a few eggs and put the penguin and the eggs outside the apartment door of the woman on the floor below. She didn't say anything for two days, so we assumed her either humorless or dead and collected them and brought them back up for future projects, possibly in Central Park.

Another time Marlyn came home on a crosstown bus with two lifelike Indian torsos. Some of the limbs had been broken off, but the bodies were a realistic and attractive reddish-brown and the heads bore excellent black wigs and had beady black eyes. People avoided Marlyn on the bus when she sat in a front seat between the torsos. Eventually they got in our way, and Marlyn took them back by cab, but not before we had broken off one of the remaining arms for a souvenir.

The arm was a marvelous accessory for a New York apartment. When company was due, we would stick it partway up the fireplace flue, so that it hung down enticingly from the elbow. Or we would wedge it behind a sofa cushion so that it appeared to be reaching up mysteriously from the sofa springs. One morning during a wild brunch party we took it out on our little balcony, which overlooked Madison between 68th and 69th streets, and wedged it between the wrought-iron railings so that it appeared to be suspended over the sidewalk. Then we forgot about it.

Two days later our doorbell rang at 8 A.M. as we prepared to leave for work. We buzzed open the intercom and heard a gruff New York voice announce, "New York Police here. Buzz us up, please."

I was still in my underwear and locked myself in the bathroom. Ann, the only one dressed, admitted two of New York's Finest. Listening through the door, I heard one say, "You gotta body on that balcony, right?"

Ann blanked out for a minute and then remembered. "Oh, no SIR!" she cried in her lovely Virginia accent. "It's just an arm."

Long pause. "An arm?"

"Oh, I'll show you! It's just an arm my roommate brought home from work!"

The police examined the plaster of Paris arm and muttered, "Yeah, well, don't put it out there again. We had a lotta complaints about this."

We heard them laughing and saying "Jeez," as they went down the stairs, and Ann rushed over to the bathroom door to tell me joyously, "Better than our wildest dreams!"

Another fine accessory that came to us from the museum, thanks to Marlyn's alertness, was a pair of life-size photographs on plyboard of men in their underwear. These were not just any men: they were, respectively, Japanese and Filipino and were part of a display that showed how the American military had used big photographs to help their men in the Pacific tell the difference between different Asian features.

Naturally these were irresistible as interior decoration, and at first we kept them up on a prominent living-room wall. Eventually this palled and we realized the photographs would make fine bedboards for the double-decker bunk beds Marlyn and Ann used. We stuck one under each mattress and forgot about it.

A few years later when we broke up housekeeping, moving men came to dismantle the bunks. When they lifted the mattresses and saw the Asian men in their underwear, there was a brief silence. Then one whispered hoarsely to the other, "Spike! Come in here and getta load-a THIS."

I would say Ann, Marlyn, and I brought out the best in each other. Another such occasion was a Christmas season when both Ann and I were working at the Metropolitan. She had been hired by the National Council office too, and it gave us the pleasant opportunity to run the mimeograph machine together, shouting "Yahoo!" when it got going fast and sounded like hoof beats.

The Metropolitan released us for the holidays only Christmas Day and December 26th, but we wouldn't have dreamed of not going home. Under these circumstances, it might have been wise of us to buy our families' Christmas gifts well in advance and mail them home but of course we were not that well-organized. Consequently, it became obvious that we would board the plane to Norfolk/Virginia Beach on Christmas Eve laden down with bags and bundles. Ann warned her mother on the telephone that this would be the case.

Mrs. Grandy said, "It wouldn't surprise me if you and Hope got off the plane dressed like Santa Claus."

Ann hung up and turned to me with a happy smile. "Do you know what my mother just said?"

I tried to talk Ann out of it. "How could we wear Santa Claus suits, Ann? When would we put them on? And where would we get them?"

"Maybe just the beards and wigs," she countered. "Let me look in the yellow pages."

On Christmas eve, carrying suitcases and shopping bags, we staggered out of the Met into a light snowfall to hail a cab to the West Side Airlines Terminal. No taxi had the slightest intention of stopping on a day like this for anyone. They roared past us, either full or displaying Off Duty signs, until one made the mistake of stopping near us at a red light. We leapt forward, threw open his door and jumped in.

"I'm off duty!" the cab driver roared. "Din't you see that sign?"

"Please," we cried, "just drop us off at the West Side Terminal on your way home. We're poor, defenseless girls on our way home to our families for Christmas. It's cold!"

"Get outta the cab!"

The light changed and he had no alternative but to start moving. Cursing creatively at the top of his lungs, he headed for the West Side. At this point, Ann said politely, "Would you mind stopping for just a minute at 43rd and Broadway? We have to pick something up."

"Are you CRAZY? Turn onto Broadway at this hour? F'GET it!"

"Oh, sir, it's the most important stop you'll ever make. Please, it's a Christmas present for a poor, sick member of my family!"

His curses reached a crescendo as he skidded onto Broadway and 43rd. Horns blared as he double-parked while Ann ran up to a second-floor wig shop. She came back in ten minutes with a huge bag and whispered to me frantically, "They cost $15 each."

As we neared the West Side Terminal, the driver's verbal abuse had reached such a pitch I began to feel alarm. I whispered to Ann, "Should we call a policeman or something? He's terrible."

"I know what," she whispered back. "Let's give him a big tip." We stared at each other in delight at this unorthodox solution. He squealed to a stop and yelled, "Okay, GEDD-OUT!" Ann handed him the fare plus a $12 tip.

The transformation was worthy of Dickens. "Holy mackerel!" he murmured. "Is that the way it is?" He jumped out of the taxi, threw open the door, grabbed all our bags and escorted us into the terminal, crying, "Merry Christmas, little ladies! Happy Noo Year! God bless you both!"

The plane for Norfolk left Newark two hours late. In Norfolk, the waiting families were simply told that we were having mechanical difficulties but it was not made clear that we hadn't left the ground yet. They were, we heard later, frozen with dread.

As we flew into Norfolk for our landing near 11 P.M., Ann and I took the huge Santa Claus wigs and beards out of the bag and put them on. They were stunning-looking with our good winter clothes and high heels and makeup. A murmur of appreciation went through the plane and sour faces began to crinkle into grins.

In those days one disembarked from planes out on the field and walked to the outdoor waiting area. As we walked towards the capacity crowd, tense and restless from waiting, a silence fell. Suddenly, a small boy giggled. And as though the dike had broken, roars of laughter and cheers of relief and applause filled the air. I have been on many a stage since then, but this was without a doubt the very best entrance I have ever made.

Life was festive in New York, and there were plenty of men to go out with, but they were not husband-type men. In the early '60s we wanted, if possible, marriages rather than relationships. My dates were fellow opera workers, wild and unpredictable singers, men who liked me but I didn't like them, and vice versa—in all, nothing to pacify my father who, on my vacations home, would tell me how all the Greek men in town were talking about the fact that Chris' daughter was fooling around wasting time in New York, disgracing the clan, instead of settling down with a decent man.

In a fit of desperation, then, I began to analyze present acquaintances in terms of possible spouse material. Did that opera singer seem a little gay? Maybe he could reform. Was that insurance broker a different religion? I would have to buck my grandmother. As I analyzed and mentally rejected the candidates, I met a soft-spoken Southern boy named Bill during a vacation at my family's beach cottage on the Outer Banks of North Carolina. Bill's family had a cottage there too, and Bill had gone to Duke—good school—and was now working in Washington—good place—and had an ear for music. He came up to New York to visit his friend Pete—still a dear friend to this day—and we all went to the Berkshires for the weekend.

It was summer and the country was gorgeous and conducive to romance. Bill seemed enamored of me and I suddenly thought, "Well, why NOT? I've got to get married and he's so CUTE and his family has a cottage near ours!"

Bill wrote me love letters after the weekend, and I went around dramatically Being In Love, holding the love letters against my chest while on the subway and staring, lips parted and eyes dreamy, at the advertisements for Dr. Scholl's foot powder.

And then I went to visit Bill in Washington. The minute I got off the Greyhound bus, I knew something had changed. Bill was absent-minded and irritable, unaffectionate and chilly. What could it be? Finally, late that first night, he sat me down and told me.

It was all right, he said, for me to be informal and casual in the country, wearing my hair down loose and dressing in simple cotton things. But when he saw me later in the city, and when in fact he had seen me just now in Washington, he was disappointed. I should be dressed more glamorously, he said. And my hair should be Done. His mother, he added, always had her hair perfectly done and was, moreover, a real lady. She would never talk as informally and, let's face it, as vulgarly as I did.

"Am I vulgar?" I cried, stricken.

Yes, he told me. When we had been driving around earlier in the day, I had said the word "barf." This, he told me, shuddering, was a shockingly vulgar word, not worthy of a lady.

I was aghast at the image I had projected. "I just meant to be funny," I whimpered. "What word should I have used?"

"Get sick," Bill said.

"But 'get sick' doesn't mean the same thing as throw up," I said.

He was appalled. "Now, that's what I MEAN! You shouldn't say 'throw up' either; it's not ladylike."

I began to feel like acting ornery. "What about 'vomit'?" I suggested.

He was apoplectic. "I don't want to hear any more words like that!" he gasped. "You just have to learn to be more elegant and ladylike, like my mother. "

And that was the end of Bill. Not long after that, I went and had my hair Done, to see if it would make me feel more ladylike. I even had my nails done. And no doubt Bill was right: the men of the '60s seemed to take notice, but oddly enough they were not the kinds of men I felt like marrying. I continued to say "Barf."

10
ANOTHER FRONT PAGE FARRELL

There comes a time, when you live and work in Manhattan, that you feel a certain craving coming on. This craving manifests itself usually after an especially unpleasant subway ride or on an evening during which one's roommates in the crowded apartment argue over the pile of dirty clothes in the closet. I call it the Cow's Navel, Nebraska, or Barren, Montana, craving.

One wishes, suddenly, desperately, to live in a town like that, not in a crowded, frantic, glamorous city of eight or nine million people. Early in 1962 I began to get that craving on a regular basis, partially because working at the Metropolitan, exotic though it was as an occupation, became more tense and frightening with every day instead of more relaxing and comprehensible.

My erratic approach to the important secretarial job certainly had a lot to do with this. How many times can one put a confidential letter into the wrong envelope and send it to the very person from whom it should be kept secret without beginning to feel a little insecure about one's abilities? The work load got ever more exhausting, too, as paperwork proliferated and the young assistant administrators grew increasingly tyrannical and bureaucratic. How well I remember those duty nights at the old Met when Bob Herman would be the administrator on duty—oh, fate worse than death!

There I would sit until midnight and later, nose running and eyes red with sties and a cold, taking letter after letter in Mr. Herman's office—such stunningly important documents as "Dear Frank: It was good to hear from you. Let's keep in touch. Sincerely, Bob." The simmering resentment of the undervalued slave began to bubble in my psyche. And lunch didn't help. You could say one thing for the Met administrators. They didn't do lunch in the traditional businessmen's manner. They saw going out to restaurants for interminable lunches a colossal waste of time and money in a crisis-ridden organization. And, though they were right, we secretaries would have relished their doing lunch out on a regular basis. Instead, I found myself doing lunch FOR them, a task I accepted as part of a good secretary's duties in those un-liberated days.

It wouldn't have been so bad if Bing had had simple tastes like Bob Herman's. Bob routinely ordered a BLT on toast with extra mayonnaise and a chocolate malted milkshake. Good, honest, American food, easy to locate in the neighborhood and hard to ruin.

But Bing would buzz me and ask me to get him half a cold roast duckling and cafe au lait. With the Burger Pit and Joe's Sandwich Shop my likely sources, Bing's order set new standards for unreasonable demand. In the half hour in which I should have been typing letters that would be screamed for later, I sat at the telephone trying to locate a restaurant on the west side of the borough that even HAD roast duckling for take-out. At last I located a Longchamps' on the upper west side, told them to hold the duck, and grabbed a subway to go get it.

Lunch was late, and the duck had the consistency of sea gull. In addition, I ruined the electric tea pot boiling milk in it for the cafe au lait. Fellow secretary Florence, sitting at her neat desk a few yards away from me, remarked, "I would never permit myself to be used in this manner." Easy for her to say. The bosses were afraid of her.

I continued to rush about preparing these wretched lunches, cursing under my breath and longing for Nebraska, until one charming gesture suddenly made it quite bearable. Paul Jaretzki, shy, worried-looking Paul, who requested for lunch nothing more than Metrecal, a 1960's diet drink, in a nice-look-ing glass, came by my desk one day, nervous and red-faced, and placed on it a gift—a Schirmer piano-vocal score of Wagner's *Die Walküre* . On the flyleaf he had written a note thanking me for being the haggard lunch woman by referring to a passage in Act One. I looked it up and noted that Hunding in that passage orders his wife to "Set the table for us!" Jaretzki's note told me I did it well. I treasure both the note and the score to this day. How productive staff members could be, I often muse, if they were told from time to time with sincerity and wit that they were doing a good job.

When my roommates finally got to the point where they avoided talking to one another and used me as a go-between, one moved out and a series of others came and went. Eventually the three-year lease on our little apartment approached its terminus. I decided that this was the time to make the break for Cow's Navel or Barren.

My four-year sojourn at the Met had been just right. There had been glamour: dressing up in satin and long gloves on opening nights, even if there was no place for staff members to sit, milling around with the billionaires and drinking champagne next to them at the Opera Club, going afterwards to Sardi's for eggs benedict. I had garnered invaluable education and operatic experience. I had anticipated the thrill of each new day in a city where I could find or do anything in the world. I had made amazing friendships and enjoyed rare opportunities—not the least of which was getting to know a nephew of the composer Richard Rodgers and dropping by the Rodgers' townhouse one evening to drink wine and play the composer's piano. Rodgers himself never knew it, but his cordial wife told us it was all right.

I could see myself getting into the rut of thinking I would never find a better place or job in my life and staying there forever, coping with heavy-duty stress and changing roommates and being reminded on occasion of my ticking biological clock, which entailed pacifying the relatives who noted it even more fiercely than I did.

Coming back home to Norfolk—I really wasn't that serious about Cow's Navel—meant finding a new job. In terms of prestigious former accomplishments, I should have been in demand. But for what? There were at that time no big cultural organizations in Norfolk, nor did I really want to be a secretary again, and this was still what most young women did.

A phone call from the San Francisco Opera gave me pause. The general director there, Kurt Herbert Adler, had heard that Bing's secretary had left. Coincidentally so had his, and he wondered if I would fly out for an interview. I had heard that Mr. Adler was appreciably more temperamental than Bing and I foresaw an even greater dosage of tension and error, despite the attractive palliative of San Francisco. I said no and wondered later if I had made a big mistake.

The Norfolk newspaper wanted to do a story about my recently-ended career in the arts. As I began to tell the details to Maureen Taylor, the wonderfully sharp editor of the women's section of the *Ledger-Star*, she handed me a sheet of paper and pointed to a typewriter. "Why don't you just write it as you're telling it?" she said.

The story appeared two days later and consisted chiefly of long quotations from my writing. A month later, Maureen called to tell me that there had been a lively argument going on at the newspaper ever since I had left. The editor-in-chief of the paper needed a secretary and had planned to ask me for an interview; Maureen wanted me for a staff reporter. I almost climbed through the phone making the choice for her. Be a secretary again? God forbid, especially since I still did not know shorthand.

But a reporter? This was a dream come true! To be one of the laid-back members of the press, smiling cynically at life's major problems, seeing my prose in print, dashing to big news events with pad and pencil! What glamour, what fulfillment!

Of course, this was the Women's Section. Papers still have them, only now they tend to call them Lifestyle or Leisure or Trends, so that women won't get insulted thinking society accuses their gender alone of liking these concepts. And some papers, in the confusion borne of the aftermath of the revolution, are reinstituting women's sections by name, following the interesting progression of subjugation/liberation/temporary equality/separatism.

Our women's pages were fun in a dopey way. We didn't know better. The higher-ups in the organization wanted us to give special coverage to the wives of civic leaders. Maureen, being a crack newspaperwoman from the liberal north, thought we should break new ground instead by focusing on more unusual women and their problems.

To illustrate this dichotomy in a perverse manner, I once made up two mock women's-page dummies, the first designed as though to please the big bosses, the second to suit Maureen's visionary taste. The first one featured huge photographs captioned, "Bank Presidents' Wives Chat in Receiving Line" and "Debutantes Take Afternoon Car Trip Through Portsmouth Tunnel." And there were stories in rich detail about tea at the Woman's Club, noting the contents of sandwiches and the dresses worn by the women who—in imitation of an actual double-entendre that had once appeared in a rural paper—"poured at both ends."

Maureen's dummy paper featured a big story with banner headlines, first of a series, entitled "Prostitutes Speak Out on Interracial Marriages," and smaller items promoting recipes heavy on garlic as an aphrodisiac. There were also mock photographs of bikini-clad women with prominent navels. The editor-in-chief at that time, notoriously conservative, disapproved of navels in public and had the staff artist air-brush them out of photographs.

An interesting aspect of writing "social news" was finding out that people misspelled their own names. Someone would send in an item stating that Treasa Williams had gotten married and her maid of honor was Shelia Parker. I would call the sender up and offer to correct the spellings of Treasa and Shelia, only to be told by the adamant mother of the bride that it certainly WAS spelled Treasa, just like it sounded, and everybody knew Sheila and Shelia were the same name.

Sometimes an item reported, "The bridegroom's mother wore a gown that fell to the floor," and we saw no reason to change so evocative a description. Of the many typographical errors we enjoyed, my favorites were "The bride's only ornament was a string of pears," and "At the reception, punch was poured by two fiends."

It was Maureen who taught me, smart-alecky English major, the difference between writing for a newspaper and for a professor. I had carefully constructed my first feature story to be a model essay, with a long and sober introductory sentence establishing the topic, a second paragraph going into the matter in a little more detail, and so on. Maureen showed me how it should be done for a newspaper by virtue of her editing job on that first story.

We used to do a feature called "Woman Behind The Man," a title abhorrent in today's social climate because it chose as subjects women whose husbands had important jobs and positions and emphasized how these good women stood behind their men and encouraged them. If such a woman did interesting things herself, it was a revelation and gave us unexpected good copy. But this was not always the case.

My assignment was to interview the wife of a man who had just been elected a regional governor of the Lions Clubs. At our meeting in her neat and modest home, I asked first, "Do you do any work outside the home, Mrs. Jones?"

"Oh, my, no. I just stay home and wait for Roy to come from work."

"Do you belong to any clubs?"

"No, I don't care for that."

"I'll bet you're a good cook, " I ventured feverishly.

"Well, I'm afraid not! We just eat real simple food. I'm not too good at anything fancy. We like to go out to cafeterias now and then."

"Aren't those pretty curtains! Do you sew?"

"Never picked up a needle in my life. I 'm just not too interested in it."

I was beginning to panic a little. "I imagine you're very help-ful to your husband in his Lions Club work, aren't you!"

"Oh, mercy, no, I stay right out of that. Roy doesn't want me interfering in his Lions work. Sometimes I go on Ladies' Night."

"Do you play bridge or cards with other ladies?"

"I don't think too much of cards. Nor of gambling."

This is my first big story, I thought. My first big story. Desperately I came up with one more question. "Do you have any pets?"

Mrs. Jones simpered a little. "Well, we don't now. But once upon a time we had a little pig. I don't think you need to put that in the paper."

I grasped at the life preserver. "A pig? Oh, that's WONderful! Did . . . did you keep it outside?"

"Heavens, no, that's against the law in this neighborhood. " Giggle. "We kept it in the bathtub. But I don't think people would be interested in that."

"Oh yes, they WOULD, Mrs. Jones!" I cried. "Do you mind if I put that in the article?

She hesitated only a moment. "Oh, that's all right, go on and put it in. But just don't make too much out of it, don't you know."

When I got back to the newspaper office, I sat down to write the deathless, Pulitzer-caliber story of Mrs. Jones standing behind Mr. Jones. In deference to her wishes, I mentioned the pig in a modest paragraph towards the end of the story. Maureen took my copy and read it, brow furrowed, making an occasional brief mark with her waxy red pencil. Suddenly, with a great gesture, she encircled a sentence and transposed it dramatically to the top of the first page with a long, red line. "This is your lead," she said.

The pig? "Oh,no, please!" I cried. "She said not to make too much out of it."

"Did she say not to use it? No? Then, it's your lead. It's the only remotely interesting thing about her in the story."

Someone else wrote the headline, following the usual newspaper procedure of concocting a headline from the first paragraph. Since the pig was in the first sentence, the headline read something like "Pig In Tub Brightens Lion's Den." Now I knew what newspaper reporting was all about.

11
STAYING IN PRINT

Maureen was good about letting me write off-the-cuff fool-ishness from time to time, so that I could keep the old creative spark alive. A few years later, after I was married and had three children, I longed for a way to get my name in print again. By then, alas, Maureen had moved to another city, but good friends in editorial positions in the paper gave me the chance by dint of a weekly little-bit-of-everything column, "Where There's Hope." The title was the idea of the late mar-velous Clarence Walton, then editor of the *Norfolk Virginian-Pilot* 's Sunday commentary section. It's a title I use for writing and speaking to this day. I could write on any topic I chose in my Sunday column, and I purposely avoided current issues, feeling that serious columnists were already pontificating enough about those things. Besides, I never knew for sure what my views were. Every time I think I despise a candidate or a policy, the next day's news reveals something that makes me wonder if I wasn't being hasty. Or if we wouldn't all feel differently about it in thirty years.

So I wrote about language, customs, personal family topics, pet peeves—and until the new managing editor came along and eased me out, no doubt because he couldn't figure out my point of view, I enjoyed some local notoriety. Some of the things I wrote about have sneaked into these reminiscences; other things, on rereading, seem SO DUMB I cannot imagine why they were printed in the first place. It's never much fun to read things you wrote when you were younger, even if your parents and husband did think they were marvelous at the time.

But several early columns that elicited widespread approval and merriment, for some reason, were about bathrooms. Maybe it's because nobody had ever written much about bath-rooms before. I was smitten with two aspects of that noble room—the noisiness of plumbing and my dislike of communal bathroom-going.

A college classmate had once invited me [I wrote] to spend a weekend in her family's lovely new home in Princeton, New Jersey. As she showed me to my room, she pointed out special features of construction her parents had chosen to insure themselves an atmosphere of peace, quiet, and gentility: cork tile floors that were not only attractive but noiseless under any heel, ceilings of unobtrusive acoustical material, carpeted stairs away from the nucleus of living room-kitchen activity.

"And then," said my friend with a long-suffering smile, "there are the bathrooms. Our toilets have the loudest flushes in Christendom." We all know whereof she spoke. It seems amazing that a country that could put Neil Armstrong you-know-where is unable to devise a modern plumbing system that operates less silently than Niagara Falls.

In our house the faucets, too, refuse to be outdone by their commode-ious colleagues. They turn on with horrendous, honking squeaks that wake the baby, alert the dog next door and give me the chalk-scraping willies.

Perhaps the most appalling example of plumbing din exists in the modern hospital. Here we find the intensive-care unit, silent and gleaming, signs everywhere urging visitors to speak in whispers. Suddenly, someone flushes. Walls crumble, mirrors fall, lamps flicker.

Another old bastion of bathroom cacophony is the luxury hotel. Guests coughing up a month's salary for the privilege of all this splendor wearily put out the Do Not Disturb sign, draw the curtains across the picture window and climb into the cool, silky sheets for an elegant and expensive night's rest.

At that moment, the guest in the adjoining luxury suite decides to take a bath. The resultant grinding, clanging, thrashing and thundering sounds through the wall suggest nuclear attack and fling the wretched neighbor sobbing and frustrated from the sack.

My favorite story about noisy plumbing concerns a young opera singer at Tanglewood, the Boston Symphony's summer music camp. The director of the opera workshop told me how this talented soprano had to sing a role that included a long and difficult unaccompanied passage. A woodwind in the orchestra provided her the pitch and she proceeded solo from there.

One night, the singer launched abruptly into the passage without waiting for her woodwind cue. Worse, she started singing four notes too high. The conductor waved his hands at her frantically to no avail. In a moment, she realized her mistake as the musical phrases became too high for her voice. She burst into tears and the curtains were closed.

The conductor ran backstage to find her sobbing in the wings. "What happened?" he cried. "Why didn't you wait for the pitch?"

"The oboe GAVE me the pitch," she cried, "and it was wrong! He gave me a high note that was wrong."

"But he didn't! You started singing before he even played."

At this juncture in the argument, someone back in the ladies' dressing room flushed a toilet. As the cheerful old commode filled, it gave forth a shrill, piercing, "Eeeeeeeeee."

"That's it!" cried the soprano. "That's the pitch I heard!"

You never know where your pitch will come from in an opera house...

My other bathroom column dealt with the peculiar social predilection of women to go *en masse* to the bathroom. I noted that it always unsettled me when, as I rose from a restaurant table with purse in hand to head for the ladies' room, five other women would leap to their feet clamoring, "Going to the ladies' room? We'll go with you."

There we went, clumping noisily across the dance floor, all eyes in the room riveted upon us. Everyone in the place knew where we were going. And what would happen when we got there? We had to chat, even when situated in separate booths. Did men go through this peculiar ceremony at men's room time? I doubted it.

I surmised that this fetish must have long-standing historical roots from rural families. Nobody would want to travel alone at night out into the dark to a spooky privy, correct? Maybe people elicited companionship in the olden days out of terror of spiders and ghosts, and it has become a striking holdover into modern times, only now people say "I'm going to go powder my nose. Wanna come with me?"

Simple facts of physical life were always a fine source of column material, an example being burps and sneezes. That column noted that, as I stopped by the newspaper office one afternoon to deliver articles, I heard the Sunday editor sneeze, "Ah-VRAKH!" I wouldn't have given the matter another thought had not the woman across the hall caught the bug at the same moment and sneezed, literally, "Ah-choo, ah-choo, ah-CHOO!"

I hurried over to her. "Did you really, honestly, say 'Ah-choo' just now when you sneezed?" She remarked that she would scarcely consider sneezing any other way. The more I thought about it, the more interesting it seemed. And it might not, I mused, be all that far-fetched because I myself say , literally, "HIC-cup!" when I hiccup. But most sneezes are not as easy to spell as hers.

My father's sneeze was legendary. He snorted, "Broo-CHOW!" If the grandchildren were around, he would extend it to "Broo-chow-chow-CHOW!" in an effort to get a rise out of them. At first they used to jump up and down in delight but, as they became older and more blasé, they would murmur vaguely, "Papou sneezed," and go on with their games.

Although my father's broo-CHOW had been known to fell a floor lamp, he disapproved of too loud a sneeze on the part of another. For years my mother stifled her sneezes into a strangled, "Rukh", hoping he wouldn't hear. Then, as the women's rights movement came into its own, she read that it was not only assertive but healthier to let the old sneeze out with gusto. Accordingly she would bellow "Ah-RAKH!" with the best of them, causing my father to thrash apoplectically out from behind his newspaper to shout "Hah? What? What happened?"

I myself like an assertive sneeze. There is something abnormal to me about a gentle "pip" into a handkerchief. I enjoy embellishing my sneezes with an international flavor. Some days I choose Russian composers: "RachMANinoff!" I sneeze. "TchaiKOFFsky!" Or "GLINka!"

As for geographical sneeze sounds, when I first learned that there was a Hawaiian island called OAHU, I realized that this was a sneeze just waiting to happen.

All of which reminds me of a woman I knew in college who burped "OP'ra glasses!" I was fascinated. Some people may consider burps an indelicate topic, but I have heard that in some countries a generous burp at the dinner table is the highest compliment that can be paid the hostess.

In any case, some talented individuals can burp at will. I have never had this talent and, in fact, cannot even burp against my will. Only once was I betrayed in this respect, and that was on an occasion in the Vassar College library.

There I sat in the decorous, stained-glass silence of the reserve book room, surrounded by dozens of stony, meditative readers turning pages silently. All of a sudden I was aware of a ticklish sensation in my throat, and I remember thinking, "Now, if I had ever been known to burp, this would probably be a burp about to come forth." But since I had never burped, I assumed it would be a yawn and opened my mouth accordingly.

"BURP!!" I roared, at a volume unparalleled in grossness, sending reserve books flying to the floor, shattering stained-glass panes, causing fellow students to fall from their chairs.

I have never been able to do it again. But you should hear me sneeze in church.

An equally interesting source of topics in my early newspaper columns was pet peeves. How writers love to share these irritations with the general public, hoping to find a kindred soul! My husband and I discovered early in our marriage that we were both peeved by long waits for something spectacularly advertised in advance. In particular, we don't like to wait for the Monster.

Anyone who enjoys an occasional grade-B monster movie will agree that most horror films put you through a slow-moving hour of boring exposition and romantic claptrap before rewarding you with the morsel you have been waiting for since the beginning—the first appearance of the monster.

This was brought home to us by a late movie on television entitled "Valley of the Gwangi" which we stayed up to watch because of the provocative sentence in the TV guide describing the plot: "Prehistoric monster escapes from rodeo."

The show began at 11:30 at night and I predicted, "We won't see a monster before 12:30." I was right. There were love scenes, rodeo acts, character development, cowboy chases, and meaningful glances for one full hour before the producers gave us what we had stayed up for—the elderly archeologist's gasp of "By George! It's a triceratops!"

As my husband shook his fist at the screen around 12:15 and shouted "Monsters!" I remarked that this was almost as bad as waiting for dinner to be served in a New York career person's apartment.

To the best of my memory, I was never served dinner before 10 P.M. in any single person's apartment in New York in all the years I worked there. People were always invited for seven o'clock but somehow food never appeared before ten. I remember gorging potato chips by the fistful, running eagerly to the kitchen from time to time to shout, "Can I help?" or "Smells mighty good in there!" even when nothing smelled.

Preliminary remarks at banquets are aggravating, too. The program promises entertainment, but first someone says, "Before we proceed to our entertainment…" and you're doomed.

You also wait horribly for the important part of the political convention—THE nomination. It's so boring to recount what one is put through on that occasion that I cannot even write it; I would fall asleep. It is very much like the audience's wait for the featured star at a concert in a coliseum. Terrible groups come on first and play for hours at top volume until one is too numb to hear the celebrity.

Perhaps our impatience in the waiting game comes of being Americans used to wide spaces and quantity. Europeans, especially eastern ones, have long since resigned themselves to queues and waits, which they bear with the patience borne of old and experienced civilization. So I'll just hush and wait for the monster. It's civilized.

One of my greatest sources of material was—and still is—my family. Speaking of monsters, a particularly popular column was about the madness that takes over our household on Halloween night. We have always felt strongly that Halloween is more a night for the fun of spookiness than for candy, no doubt a holdover from my own childhood, in which no one had yet heard of Trick or Treat.

There is no mere humdrum giving out of treats at our front door. As far as we are concerned, Halloween is meant to be scary and small fry coming in costume to our threshold deserve, and get, the full treatment.

My husband dresses like Frankenstein, pencils a fierce scar across his face, occasionally covers his eyes with small white scallop shells from the beach, and laughs. You have never heard a laugh equal in horror to his Frankenstein parody.

I fish my college academic gown out of mothballs. Its voluminous blackness is splendid and batlike over a pair of dark tights, and I let down my hair, put black smudges under my eyes and powder my face stark white. Lips outlined in dark green are a nice touch, and I hold a candle. For variety, I sometimes put my hair over my face and perch a pair of glasses on top.

We construct monsters and ghosts on the sofa and living-room chairs and forsake electricity for flickering candle stubs. When the little shavers arrive to trick or treat, we invite them in. Our own kids, when small, were delighted by the production, forgetting that they too were entitled to go out and collect sacks full of delicacies.

The trouble with a show like this is that word spreads as the evening progresses. As curfew approaches and supplies dwindle, the crowds burgeon about our house. Youngsters return bringing friends, shrieks and screams attend the opening of the door, cars stop in the street with motors running and wait to see the spectres.

Before we bought a house, my husband and I went faithfully every Halloween to my mother's, to assist her with her horror show. Hers was better than ours, really, for her house sat back amid tall, dark trees and trick-or-treaters had to come down a long driveway. It was very effective to station Frankenstein behind a tree partway down the drive and have him stagger out, snarling, from time to time.

When I was a kid, nobody went around getting candy. Mainly we had parties. My parents put on a humdinger every year, at which the foundations were laid for the full-scale show I now mount annually in my own home. Once, my mother herded a group of us, ages nine and ten, into the dark front bedroom where Daddy lay supine on the bed, eyes closed, covered by a sheet under which he held a flashlight aimed at his chin.

"This is a famous Egyptian king, Tutankhamen," intoned Mama. "He has been asleep for 2000 years and tonight, when the clock strikes twelve, he will wake up." This was the cue for my cousin Stacey, in the adjoining bathroom, to commence striking the dinner gong. At the 12th stroke, my father let out a horrible roar, flailed his arms and legs about and tossed sheet and flashlight to the winds.

We children gave unanimous voice to one huge scream of terror, bolted for the hall and fell down the steps. Best Halloween any of us ever had. I note that there's a movement afoot in some churches, mine included, to condemn the spooks of Halloween for Demonic Influence and to induce kids to dress like saints or angels instead. I really think the church fathers have misinterpreted the fun this time and looked for the devil in the wrong place.

Though I began working at the paper before I was married, the column, having had its beginnings after our kids were born, dealt frequently with the children. In one piece, I confessed to a lingering dislike for swimming pools:

I finally got the kids into the ocean the other day, I wrote, and I am happy to report that they liked it so well they might forget for a week or two about going to pools.

For the past couple of summers, they have had a love affair with pools, but no ordinary pools. These must be large and cement and far from home. They will not touch on a bet the little plastic splash-pond we bought hopefully at the beginning of the summer and had delivered to our back yard.

In desperation, I myself fill it with the hose from time to time, put on a bathing suit and go out and sit in it, reminding myself of a mother whale sitting in a plastic dish pan. "Look, kids!" I shriek, splashing the water with hysterical enthusiasm and kicking my feet. "Isn't this FUN and COOL?" They watch me sullenly and run to stand by the car, chanting, "Take us to a cement pool."

There are a few cement pools I could take them to, I guess, but I try to get out of it for a purely selfish and neurotic reason. I don't like Floating Things.

Maybe there are pools in the vicinity that do not have bugs or hair floating in them, but it has not been my good luck to patronize them. The hair is worse than the bugs, I think, and you can smell the chlorine.

For some of these same queasy reasons, I prefer ocean to bay, because in any calm body of water there are likely to be floating things. The ocean is big and tough and won't put up with too much of it, and that powerful salty spray at least seems purer, although society is attempting eagerly to undermine it with dumpings of chemicals and garbage.

Perhaps the only pool I ever really respected in my life was the one that existed at Natural Bridge resort in the Virginia mountains. It was down near the restaurant and souvenir shop, a small cement pool but one with a charmingly natural, stone-hewn look as though it had been discovered centuries before. Its particular charm was that it was fed by an ice-cold mountain stream that poured in at one side and flowed out the other. I don't know what sort of filter system it had, but the water was so cold that one couldn't help but figure that filtering and drains were unnecessary.

I don't remember much in the way of floating objects in that pool. Perhaps too few people could brave the ice, and less traffic meant less debris. Until I get up there some day to check its properties again, I will avoid pools and try to steer the group to the ocean, preferably on a day when the water is not too calm.

When trying to think each week of a column topic, I became introspective and personal. It was because of this that I produced a column about phobias which was headlined "A Mother's Garden of Fears."

Lately, I wrote, I seem to read a lot about phobias. The varieties are fascinating—acrophobia, agoraphobia, gephyrophobia, arachnophobia. The four I have just mentioned are particular phobias of mine, and in case these terms are not as yet household words in your families, I translate gladly: fear of heights, fear of the marketplace, fear of bridges, fear of spiders.

The word "phobia" is pretty strong when taken at serious psychological face value. A true acrophobic would refuse to go up into the Empire State Building or in an airplane. A sincere gephyrophobic would take a fifteen-mile detour to avoid driving over a narrow bridge.

I am not that far gone, but I confess to a certain uneasiness in all these categories. I note, too, that my phobias have grown more intense since I have become a mother. Fear of the children's possible doom paralyzes me and turns me into a jellified neurotic, for example, at my aunt's seventeenth floor apartment.

"Want to come out on the balcony and look at the harbor, children?" someone asks my brood.

"No, " I gasp, "no!", so weak with fear that I am unable to raise my voice to an audible level, as in a nightmare.

"Now, don't be silly," another relative admonishes. "We won't let them climb over the railing. You're just giving them your fear."

"Exactly!" I croak hoarsely, my knees buckling. "I WANT them to have my fear; it's my legacy to them! Suppose they DO start to climb over? You can't just say 'No-no, dear,' as though they've picked up a wad of chewing gum. This is MUCH more serious, it's. . . ."

"Nonsense," smiles everyone tolerantly, taking the kids out onto the balcony and closing the door. I turn my face to the wall, hyperventilating. In a moment, they all come back in, cheerful and refreshed. Does this cure me of my unreasonable phobia—which is in fact fear of <u>ledges</u>, not heights? No.

The word "agoraphobia" has come to mean fear of crowds, but the original word "agora" meant marketplace. I stick to the original. This <u>fear</u> comes on me only at the prospect of entering a decorator showroom full of breakable and pristine objects in the company of small children. Or of dropping into yet another of the hundreds of huge discount stores that all sell the same tons of shoddy goods, over-manufacturing at its worst.

As for gephyrophobia, the fear of bridges, never again will I take small children over that cursed Treasure Island swinging bridge at the Botanical Gardens, where some smart-alecky tourist always begins to jump up and down to make the bridge sway. Nor do I happily drive over huge, high-span bridges with low railings. One false move, I tell you, and. . . .

And, finally, there is my irrational arachnophobia—the morbid fear that draws me inexorably to the window every five minutes to see if that big, horrendous, black-and-yellow spider is still in its web over by the garage. I know that most spiders are kindly souls who eat bugs, I know I loved reading *Charlotte's Web* as much as everybody else, yet I still blanch at the cheerful music of a tarantella, knowing that the word is based on—you've got it—TARANTULA, the sum of all my horrors.

Once I had a yellow silk scarf with glossy black tassels on the ends. On a windy ride, one of the tassels flew forward and settled on my shoulder. I glimpsed it out of the corner of my eye, took it at once for a giant spider, and, shrieking, hit the roof of the car so hard with my head we debated trading it in. The car, not my head.

Currently I am inventing words for new, private phobias. For this I must go back to the ancient Greek roots of vocabulary. Afraid of elevators as I am? You've got anypsoterephobia.

You're scared of yourself in a bathing-suit? No problem, you're a loutrorouchophobic. And you try to avoid sad movies? Well, that would be lyperokinematophobia.

And by now you're afraid to read any more columns? Let's see, that ought to be . . . .

12
LOOKING FOR
COMRADE GOODBAR

During the few years fresh from New York when I worked at the newspaper office, before marrying and writing the column from home, I found to my surprise that there was no scarcity of social life. There were some six single men in town and only two or three "interesting" single women, so we women were in demand. Little by little, for reasons even I never understood, I mentally eliminated the available men from my list of possible spouses, although I'm sure in retrospect that a solid and pleasant marriage could have been promoted and arranged with some of them.

It was to avoid one persistent caller in particular that I decided to tie up a few evenings a week by taking a course. In fact, an article in a woman's magazine emphasized this as the perfect way to meet promising men. "They will have the same intellectual interests as you," the writer noted, and similar intellectual interests were not low on my list of priorities.

In fact, my criteria for a good mate were, I felt, relatively simple. He had to have a good sense of humor and not be too cynical. Under no circumstances should he know or care more about fashion or house decor than I did. I wanted him to want children and to be easy on them. He had to love to eat and not be picky about it. And his feet must absolutely be larger than mine.

But I never really expected to find this Prince Charming at an evening class. I thought the class would simply provide a little intellectual stimulation and perhaps a new addition or two to my circle of Norfolk friends. I went out to Old Dominion University, Norfolk's urban institution of higher learning, and looked through the evening college catalog. There, suddenly, was a subject I had always wanted to study but hadn't had time—Russian language.

Now here, I thought, is a subject that is likely to attract fellow students of a provocative make-up: men in belted trench coats, hats and sunglasses. Men with unusual Eastern European accents. Spies, with whom Virginia Beach used to be loaded before the Cold War ended. The first meeting of the class showed that about eighteen men and four women had enrolled. I deemed this a perfect ratio.

Of the men, five were retired military commanders, curiously waiting until retirement to learn the language of the enemy. Another was an elderly Portuguese naval officer. One lieutenant, too young for me anyway, was gay. A serious civil servant was apparently happily married and the father of six, and the others were such as to elude my memory even today. Any married ones were definitely off limits, since in those days they didn't recycle men the way they do now. The other three women were there for the reason I was: they had read the same article.

I soon decided that the lack of potential bridegrooms was irrelevant because the course was interesting. But a girl named Shirley, who always sat next to me, had kept her goals in sight. During the third class session she nudged me vigorously in the ribs.

"The professor is single."

"You're kidding," I whispered. "He looks older than we do. How many times has he been married?"

"I heard he's never been married."

"NEVER MARRIED?" We stared at him as he wrote on the blackboard, lecturing loudly enough to drown out our whispers. "Well, there must be something the matter with him then. Let's watch how he holds the chalk."

He turned to meet our fixed gazes. There was something pleasant-looking about him even if he didn't have the all-American preppie look we usually looked for in dates in those days. His haircut reminded me of the actor Stewart Granger and he had a cheerful, ruddy face. Apparently he had sensed the gist of our conversation.

"Took me long time to get out of Soviet Union," he said suddenly, omitting the articles in his speech as Russians tend to do. "Now at last I am American citizen, I have two college degrees, this is my first job and I am free to look for wife."

At this, Shirley crossed her legs in the most unusual manner I had ever seen. My mind worked feverishly as I kept a nervous eye on her. Suddenly an inspiration hit me. I thought, "The man is as good as mine. He's a Russian and I'm a Greek. This means we have the same Easter."

Instantly I made mental plans to invite him to Greek Easter dinner at my grandmother's house. Easter was a long way off yet, but I figured I could be as charming as possible and make good grades until Lent and then spring the invitation on him.

As fall progressed into winter, we learned ever more fascinating things about the professor. First of all, his name was Larry H. McReed. Now this was, admittedly, peculiar. After my initial disappointment at thinking I had drawn some American graduate student for a Russian teacher, I heard his Russian accent. He explained to the class at our first meeting that his name, before he changed it, was Leonid Mihalap.

As a teen-aged boy in Bobruisk, Byelorus, he learned German in high school. This eventually saved his life. His mother, a Red Army nurse, went to war, becoming a highly-decorated officer rising to the rank of lieutenant colonel. His only sister was away in medical school. His father, the manager of a small factory, was too old to be drafted. But it would not be long before Leonid himself was the right age for the draft and would have to fight for Stalin.

If there was anything less appealing to young Leonid and his father than fighting for Stalin, it would have been hard to imagine. Though his mother was a candidate for Communist Party membership, his father was a passive resister, well aware of Stalin's atrocities to his own people.

As the war progressed, father and son heard—incorrectly, as it turned out—that his mother had been killed in action. In addition, they were told that Leonid's sister had been lost as well. Thinking they were the only two family members left, Leonid and his father discussed the future.

"One of us has to survive," his father said. They knew the likelihood was good that young Leonid would die in battle or invasion if he were to stay in the Soviet Union. They decided on a plan. His father, assuming that he was a widower, would remarry and have more children to carry on the family name. Leonid would find a way to get out of the Soviet Union. Somehow, the name would go on.

In 1941, the German Army entered Bobruisk. Many Soviet citizens in those times considered the Germans a lesser evil than Stalin. They knew little or nothing about the Nazi party, nor about Hitler's vicious intentions. All they knew at this point was that somebody was fighting against Stalin, a man who slaughtered his own people, and that this presented an opportunity.

It was agreed that Leonid should join the invading German army as an interpreter. This was not an unusual idea. Leonid tells us now that many thousands of Soviet citizens at first welcomed the German Army as liberators, greeting them in the villages with bread and salt in the Russian tradition of hospitality.

On an August morning in 1943, Leonid's father kissed him on both eyes and told him goodbye. He instructed him to write—just once—when he had gotten safely out of the Soviet Union and to include a special coded message to indicate whether or not he was being treated humanely by the German Army. After that, they agreed, they would not attempt to communicate with one another—ever again.

Leonid, treated well by the Germans, retreated with them through the Soviet Union. He considered it his personal mission to save as many of his countrymen's lives as possible, and this he did by calling out advice and instructions in Russian to villagers as his German unit approached. Before long, he wrote the promised letter to his father.

It was the goal of Russian boys like Leonid to liberate their country from Communism and, at the same time, to be free of a monster like Hitler. Many of them had heard of the Russian Liberation Army, unique troops formed and being trained under the leadership of a former Soviet general, Vlassov. Their goal, as they trained in Germany, was to go back into their country to fight the Stalin regime.

At the end of the war Leonid finally located, with the help of the Germans, a Vlassov training school for commissioned and non-commissioned officers. In April 1945, he and his fellow trainees, while retreating from the advancing Soviets, were interned by the Third U.S. Army. Soldiers like Leonid, in German uniform with patches of the Russian Liberation Army, were clearly not Germans and were a puzzle to the Americans, who kept them in internment camps until they could decide what to do with them.

What happened to most of these brave young men is a black page in American history. At Yalta, President Roosevelt and Prime Minister Churchill acceded to Stalin's demand that such men be "returned home" to be dealt with. Indeed they were dealt with. Execution was probably, for them, the pleasantest way Stalin found to deal with them. But some of them didn't get sent home. Among the lucky ones was Leonid, who was serving as interpreter in the prisoner of war camp for the American Counter Intelligence officer assigned to the camp. He told the officer, in German, that he was of German extraction. Knowing he lied and understanding the reason for it, the wise young officer discharged him before he could be forcibly repatriated.

And now over twenty years had elapsed since those harrowing days. Leonid, having joined the American Army in postwar Germany, got to the United States. In Fort Dix, New Jersey, he contemplated changing his name so that the Soviets might have a hard time finding him if ever Stalin sent over a personal assassin, a grandiose but not unusual concept for someone who had lived under Stalin's government.

He went to the movies, a war movie, and the hero's name was Larry Reed. This sounded splendid to the young Russian.

The next day he went to a lawyer and said, "I want to be Larry Reed."

The lawyer said, "Just pay my fee and you can be anything you want."

"But my friends in the Army call me 'Mac'," said Leonid.

"No problem," said the lawyer. "We'll put Mac in front of the Reed. McReed."

"McReed?" repeated Leonid. "Is this American?"

"As American as apple pie."

Having no idea that he was christening himself with a nickname and becoming Scotch or Irish to boot, Leonid paid his $123 and became Larry H. McReed. The H stood for Harold. When he was discharged from the army, he went to Georgetown University on his G.I. Bill for a bachelor's and master's. And his first teaching job turned out to be Old Dominion University in Norfolk. I was in his class. Not only that, Shirley and I were looking him over as a potential mate.

As Lent approached, I invited Larry McReed to Greek Easter Dinner. Delighted at the prospect of social life—he had lived alone for a long time—he accepted, and I picked him up and brought him to Yaya's house after midnight services Easter Saturday night.

There are two Greek Easter dinners. The first one takes place at about 3 A.M., after church. Having fasted from meat and dairy products during Easter Week, the Greeks are not about to wait too long before having dinner on Easter. Right after midnight service is good enough for them. Three A.M. dinner at Yaya's house was a fabulous celebration—roast lamb, baked livers with fennel and onion, homemade bread, cheese and olives, wine, all this accompanied by raucous conversation and laughter and hymns.

No wonder lonesome Larry looked happy. We hadn't invited him to the 5 P.M. dinner later in the day, but it didn't matter. He was with a family.

I waited for the professor to ask me out in the weeks after Easter dinner, but he didn't. Not only that, he seemed to be avoiding my glance in class. Now, thirty years later, we realize that he was scared. This was obviously a single girl he might want to marry, but how dared he proceed? She was an only child, an only niece, an only grandchild, with a large, over-bearing family. He was, in fact, too scared to proceed.

He denies it, but I suggest he was also stunned by the noisy way we ate and drank that night. He, as a Russian who had lived alone for years, ate in silence, plowing diligently through his plate until everything was eaten and only then looking up to make conversation. We Greeks, on the other hand, filled our mouths full of food and talked through it, spitting, usually inadvertently, from time to time. Maybe we had grossed him out.

Loath to give up on him so soon, I decided to try for an A in his course that he would never be able to ignore. When the final grades came out in May, I had a 97 average. He still didn't call me up.

"Forget him, then!" I thought. "I don't need to keep taking Russian. Maybe I should switch to something like Industrial Arts this September. That ought to bring lots of macho brutes out of the woodwork."

In mid-August, my telephone rang. It was the Russian professor. He said, without preliminary conversation, "Can you come to dinner Tuesday night?"

"I think so." I felt a tremor of premonition.

"Can you cook?" he added. "I have a chicken."

I suspected the chicken might be alive and in a crate, and he would say, "If you are real woman, you can wring chicken's neck and pluck feathers."

But I accepted the invitation and then went to report this to my parents.

"I won't be home for dinner Tuesday night. I'm going to the Russian teacher's apartment for dinner."

My father was scandalized. "To his APARTMENT?" He turned to my mother. "How old is she now?"

My mother said, "Twenty-nine."

"GO AHEAD!" screamed my father.

When I arrived at the professor's apartment for dinner that Tuesday night, he met me at the door and, with a slightly confused, embarrassed look, handed me a drink. Then he said, "Chicken is in kitchen."

Fortunately, the chicken was dead. He watched for a few minutes as I prepared it for baking and rummaged in the refrigerator for salad fixings. Pleased, finally, that a meal was actually in progress, he said, "I'll go inside and correct papers."

He strolled nervously back and forth from living-room to kitchen as I cooked, until finally we sat down at his little dining-room table and ate the entire chicken in nearly total silence, Russian-style. We couldn't think of anything to talk about. As the meal ended, I looked at my watch. It was already six-fifteen! I stood up. "Well, maybe I should get going..."

"Don't go!" he said quickly. "Let us look at telewision."

We sat on the couch in front of his television set and I crossed my legs. He observed, "You have nice legs."

Oh-oh, I thought. I should have known things might head in this direction. My father was right in being nervous.

But his conversation took a different tack at once. "How old is your grandmother?"

My grandmother?! "She's ninety-two."

He said, "She needs great grand-child. Let's get married."

I thought, he's insane. I looked around for a possible weapon. "Are you crazy? I cooked a chicken and I took your course. Is this enough reason for us to spend the rest of our lives together?"

"Well," he said with a philosophical shrug. "I give you more reasons. We both want children, right?" I nodded. "We are both old." That was for sure.

"And," he concluded, "we are both little bit crazy. So we might as well get married. Yes or no?"

It just didn't seem right. I said desperately, "But this isn't a good proposal. You haven't said you love me!"

"I don't love you," he replied. "I barely know you."

The fact that everything he had just said was true didn't matter. I was an American and wanted ROMANCE. What did he mean, he didn't love me? How could I accept a proposal from a man who spoke such stark, unromantic truth? "But people have to love each other to get married!"

"Well, we WILL love each other," he countered. "Real love comes after marriage."

Again, this was true, but did I want to hear it? This was appallingly like an arranged marriage, except that we ourselves were apparently arranging it. I told him I would have to think it over. "Besides," I added in growing irritation, "we haven't even gone OUT."

"Gone out where?"

"On DATES! People who get married have to go out on dates first." He stared at me, confused. By now I realized in exasperation that I would have to handle this entire courtship myself. "Well, we can go out Sunday. Do you want to go to my grandmother's house for Sunday dinner?"

His face lit up. "That would be nice. Will you pick me up?"

Another irritating blow. He wouldn't even act like an escort. I said, "Yes, I'll pick you up at one o'clock!" and I headed home, sputtering in annoyance.

The rest of the week went by and my phone was silent. Finally, I called him up on Saturday night. I was angry. "Do you or do you not want to go to my grandmother's house for dinner tomorrow?"

"Yes, of course!" he said cheerfully. "I wait for you at one o'clock."

He was waiting on the sidewalk outside his apartment next day. As he climbed into my little Volkswagen, I snapped, "Why haven't you called me up all week? You asked me to MARRY you on Tuesday!"

He said pleasantly, "I don't have anything else to say. I asked you question, I wait for answer."

It took three weeks before I accepted the proposal. I made him take me out on Dates—to the movies, to the beach—and whenever he would reiterate the proposal, I would snap, "Not if you don't love me!"

Finally one night, as he dropped me at the front door—he had learned to pick me up—he countered disgustedly, "Oh, all right, all right, I love you. Is that what I am supposed to say?"

Amazed, I answered, "Well, okay then, I'll marry you."

I didn't hear from him for two weeks.

13

LEAVING THE NEST—SLOWLY

My Aunt Connie despaired of me, her only niece, seeing in me the combination of a bookish, independent father and a forward-thinking mother—a girl who ignored, as she put it, "the things all girls look forward to." I was, in fact, far less untraditional than she insisted I was; but over the years I had come to regard with some embarrassment and suspicion the things she felt all girls were supposed to look forward to.

These things included accumulation of trousseaus and dowries, expertise in washing lingerie by hand, "doing over" rooms that looked all right to begin with, going to club meetings, playing cards for supposed relaxation and social cachet with people who got mad when you played wrong, and... planning weddings.

Her frustration reached its zenith when I became engaged. First of all, she was terribly worried about my fiance. Who, after all, was he? We knew nothing about his family. He was from an enemy country and a probable spy. And he was a struggling professor who lived in a furnished apartment, lending it his own decorating flair by thumb-tacking onto the dining-room wall a calendar from Small's Hardware Store.

I thought the calendar was pleasant and didn't even take it down after we got married, until my mother whispered to me after a few months that the family was having Serious Discussions about it.

My lack of interest in my own wedding preparations had Aunt Connie near apoplexy. "Who will your attendants be?" she asked me irritably one day. "You haven't allowed yourself much time to make plans."

"Well, I thought I would just ask Ann," I replied. "She already lives right here in Virginia Beach and I thought she could just wear whatever she likes. I don't want her to go to any expense."

There was a pained silence. "What events have you planned for your out-of-town guests?"

"Out-of-town guests? Do I need to have any?"

"Honestly, sometimes I don't even think you have a mother. Hasn't your mother discussed this with you? You have a god-father and cousins in Baltimore. Are they just going to come down here and rattle around on their own?"

I wrote some things down on a list, nodding my head, trying frantically to think of a way to change the subject.

"And have you thought about what sort of shower you want? There are plenty of people eager to give you a shower."

"No, I don't want to have a shower! Showers embarrass me—all those women sitting around smiling, watching me open gifts I don't need while the wrapping paper rattles in the silence. And meantime they're all thinking that they have to buy you a wedding present too. And then we'd have to play those little games and eat sheet cake and everything. No, I real-ly don't want a shower: I've been to too many myself." I was beginning to feel brave, even though Aunt Connie could always win an argument by sounding emotional and acting like a martyr.

She heaved a prodigious sigh. "All right, go ahead and be Bohemian, darling. You're just as Bohemian as your mother."

The thought of my mother being Bohemian tickled me. Mama had had Her Wedding and Her Gifts and Her Trousseau and Her House and all those things—but somehow she wasn't pushing me to have them. In retrospect, I think she figured it had been overkill and her years of accumulation of goods were beginning to panic her. She wanted to leave them to me and it would create problems if I had stuff of my own.

But there was one traditional thing I could not escape, and Aunt Connie saw to it. She called me a week before my wed-ding, her voice trembling with irritation. "Has your mother bought you your bridal set yet?"

Bohemian though I was, I knew what a bridal set was. I had been to too many of those embarrassing showers. "Oh Aunt

Connie, I don't need a bridal set! I got tons of nylon gowns and pajamas as gifts when I graduated from college, and nylon never wears out."

Her voice fell to a hoarse whisper. "This makes me sick. You won't have a bridal shower like every normal girl would want to have, and now your own mother, *my sister*, won't even buy you a bridal set—every girl's wedding dream come true."

In my panic, I began to get stubborn. "Aunt Connie, it doesn't MATTER. I know dozens of girls who had showers and bridal sets and now they're all getting divorced."

"Don't be sarcastic," Aunt Connie snapped. "You're the only daughter in the entire Christopoulos family. Girls from little NOTHING families have showers and bridal sets, and you're a Christopoulos. If your own mother won't buy you a bridal set, I'll have to do it. Meet me at Rice's Bridal Salon Monday on your lunch hour."

Rarely have I faced an appointment other than wisdom tooth extraction with greater dread. Trying on clothes before a jury consisting of Aunt Connie and Southern saleswomen was a terrifying prospect at the best of times. To try on bridal sets was an ordeal of horrifying proportions.

Some women—perhaps Marilyn Monroe or Jayne Mansfield—might have looked good in the bridal sets. I thought I looked like a Coke bottle. Nylon clings and shines through, and there's nothing to hide your shape. In stunned embarrassment, I paraded in the see-through garments before the jury, who cocked their heads and sighed dramatically and said, "Oh, isn't she just a dream come true!"

I kept rejecting the gossamer offerings until, by 3 P.M., we hit the Naivette Shoppe, one of the more expensive boutiques, where shoppers sat on soft couches and were served coffee while saleswomen who knew who you were went to a back room and "brought things out."

The fourth thing they brought out was a pale blue and white lace creation, a nightgown with little spaghetti straps and its matching negligee. I looked at the price tag: $89.95 (this was

1964), ten dollars more than the monthly rent of Larry's apartment, which we would be struggling together to pay in just a few short weeks.

"Don't you like this one, dawlin'? Just tell me what's wrong with this one," crowed the saleswoman.

"Well, I'm just flat-chested and this sort of brings that out."

"Dawlin', we can DO something about that! If that's all that worries you, I'll just take it back to alterations and they can stuff some nylon net right HEAH and HEAH, and you'll look just beautiful."

Stuffing a nightgown. But if it would shorten the ordeal, why not? I consented, Aunt Connie wrote a check and they rushed back to alter the bosom of the bridal set.

We went to a nearby luncheonette for coffee. Aunt Connie's brow was furrowed. "Do you like that bridal set, darling? You don't really look happy to me."

"Oh, I love it, I love it!" My hand shook as I poured cream in my coffee.

She sighed again. "Well, you know he loves you no matter what you wear."

"I guess so," I said.

"What do you mean, you GUESS so?"

"Well, he doesn't like to say he loves me. He says real love comes later."

"He DOESN'T LOVE YOU?" Her face was pale.

I thought, Why in the name of God have I gotten myself into this truthful discussion? When will I learn to lie at the right time? I tried to patch it up. "Well, don't you think he's right? I mean, I know he LIKES me, but it might not be the truth to say he LOVES me, when after all . . . ."

She could hardly speak. "This makes me sick . . . this makes me SICK. A man we barely know, no bridal set, and all you know is he 'likes' you."

My efforts to recover were futile. I laughed and tried to lie. "Oh, I bet you he really DOES love me, tee-hee, yes, he really IS romantic, I just don't talk about it much, oh, you know how it is, ha-ha . . . ."

But she knew. She knew. And her eyes were glazed with fear and disappointment.

We were married on Thanksgiving Day, 1964, which meant we really didn't need to have a reception—another untraditional shock—because everybody was going to go home to a private Thanksgiving dinner anyway, as we did with the wedding party. And then Larry and I left for our weekend honeymoon—to a glamorous newlywed location? Heavens no, my parents' beach cottage in North Carolina was vacant and free, even though it would be cold there.

Ill at ease with one another, terrified at the step we had just taken, we arrived at the beach house in the cold dark. In a burst of awkward romantic tradition, Larry tried to carry me over the threshold but I weighed more than he had anticipated. Nonetheless, flushed a little with the unexpected romance of that, I took my suitcase into the icy bedroom and opened it. There lay the bridal set. Larry was in the living-room trying to start a fire in the fireplace.

I suddenly thought, This has to be the dumbest moment of my life so far. What do I SAY when I walk into the cold living-room in this nightgown and negligee? There has to be a line for this scene, but no matter WHAT the line is, it's going to be embarrassing. How can it not be embarrassing?

As I pulled on the scratchy-bosomed pale blue gown, I rehearsed sample entrance lines: "Hey, look at these nylon BOSOMS." Or, "Hiya, big boy," with my teeth clenched like Mae West. No, how about, "Oh, dawlin', ah've been waitin' for this moment awl my life," followed by emotional sobs. Here I had been a performer already for years and I couldn't think of a decent, non-threatening entrance line to go with the Bridal Set.

I sidled into the living-room, hoping to get to the kitchen before he could even see me. But, no—he looked up from the hearth in time to see me in the pale blue bridal set.

Aghast, he cried, "Honey, you are going to catch COLD in dat thing! For heaven's sake, go put on sweater."

I said, "I didn't bring a sweater."

He said, "I have one in car!" And quickly he ran out to the car and found in the trunk his old Army pullover, olive-drab and stained with kerosene. He made me put it on over the bridal set and we drank champagne. I thought with pleasure of what Aunt Connie's facial expression would have been if she could have joined us.

The fact that we had just married couldn't alter a lifetime of living habits up to that point. When Larry had first moved to Norfolk and rented his little furnished bachelor apartment, one of his initial purchases was a television set. Alone except for the hours he taught class, he counted on the company provided by the TV and watched it constantly, with pleasure, while he corrected papers or ate breakfast or dinner. He still loves the tube, Ph.D. or not, and is not ashamed to admit it.

So the fact that we married on a Thursday didn't prevent him from remembering that on Friday nights one of the local channels showed old movies all night long. Larry loves old movies, particularly vintage films of the '30s and '40s and war movies of the '50s.

The moment we arrived at our honeymoon cottage in Kill Devil Hills, NC, he rushed to the television set to find that it was sending out a snowy signal and needed repair. Aghast, he cried, "How can we watch the movies tomorrow night?"

"Don't worry," I said, "I know the people at Manteo Furniture Company and I'm sure they can repair it for us."

Next morning we drove the twenty miles into Manteo and carried the TV set into the shop. There stood Mr. Wescott, whose family had run the business for as long as I could remember and still does. I said, "Mr. Wescott, do you think your people could fix this set for us so we can watch the all-night movies tonight?"

"I reckon we can," he said pleasantly. "Well now, how's your mother and daddy? Y'all down for Thanksgiving weekend?"

"No, " I said, "I'm down for my honeymoon. This is my husband, Larry McReed. We just got married yesterday."

Mr. Wescott looked at us both for a moment and then gazed at the television set. "You want this repaired for the all-night movies tonight?"

"Yes sir."

There was a long silence. "Well, I'll see if I can't get the boys to deliver it over there some time this evening." Brow furrowed, he watched us leave the furniture store.

That afternoon about 5 P.M. we heard the furniture store truck rumble up the driveway. In a moment, there were footsteps on the stairs and then a Thump as the Manteo Furniture boys set down the repaired television and knocked on the door. "Now, come on, hurry up and let's git OUTTA here!" came a hoarse whisper. And before we could open the door to greet them, they had tumbled wildly down the steps and driven off, tires screeching. Mr. Wescott had probably stood by the truck giving them a lecture: "Now, they're down here on their honeymoon, see? I don't know why in the devil they gotta have this TV tonight, but y'all set it down and DON'T BOTHER THEM NONE."

As it was, we watched movies that night until, bleary-eyed, I said to my brand new spouse, "I'm tired, I'm going to bed." At about 3 A.M., he came into the bedroom and shook me awake. What do you know, I thought, he remembered he's married and is being romantic.

"Honey!" he cried eagerly, "Greta Garbo is on in 'Ninotchka!' Quick, get up and come watch this!"

Despite these little tensions, we knew we were securely married, if for no other reason than that we had been married twice. I was born and christened Greek Orthodox long before I knew what that meant—that's how the Greeks do it—but Larry, despite his emigration from a country that had followed the Orthodox denomination since 988 A.D., had arrived in the United States unchurched. This was due, naturally, to the government under Stalin, which condemned religion and closed the churches.

But now that Larry was Larry McReed, not Leonid Mihalap, and was fairly certain he would never go again to his country of birth, he preferred not to join a church community that would remind him of his past. Instead, he chose to become Roman Catholic—similar in ritual but not soul-jarringly familiar.

Not being adamant or opinionated about religious matters, I thought this was fine and greatly enjoyed accompanying him to Mass and taking him with me occasionally to the Greek church as well. It may not have been a problem with us, but my grandmother, uncles, and aunts soon launched into a campaign to make it a major problem with everybody.

"I have heard," said our Greek priest, in a voice heavy with foreboding and grief, "that you are taking instruction in the Catholic Church. Is this true, Hope?"

"No, " I said, puzzled. "It's not true. Who would have told you a thing like that?"

"I'm not at liberty to say," he said, worriedly, though his face had YOUR RELATIVES written all over it in neon lights.

I knew it couldn't be Mama and Daddy. Daddy, pretty much on my own wave length, wouldn't have cared if we became Buddhists, as long as he didn't have to go to any services. Mama was amenable to most things but—as I was to realize later—was under constant and harrowing pressure from her side of the family.

To please everybody, we had two weddings. The Catholics, who were at that time in the midst of a liberating Ecumenical Council in Rome, told us it was perfectly all right with them for us to have a Greek wedding as well as a Catholic one, provided theirs got the newspaper publicity. The Greeks said they wouldn't stop us from having two weddings, provided theirs came first, presumably so that it would "take" with God.

At two o'clock on Thanksgiving Day, the immediate family gathered in Yaya's living room, where our good friend Father Charles performed a simple Greek Orthodox ceremony. Simple though it seemed, our attempts to get permission to have it in a home rather than the church had been complex. My father had finally obtained this permission by writing directly to the Patriarch in Istanbul, thereby insulting the American archbishop by bypassing the hierarchy. Afterward, we all drank a toast in some of Yaya's homemade wild cherry wine and then piled into cars and drove across town to Blessed Sacrament Catholic Church, where Father Ryan married us in the publicized ceremony.

Hope and Larry emerging from one of their two wedding ceremonies.

To the amazement of my relatives, I told the organist to go ahead and just play "Here Comes the Bride" instead of Bach, Purcell, or Mozart. I figured I had already upset them enough with my Bohemianism.

But did these complex arrangements please the clan? Lord, no, the subliminal and ultraliminal messages were just beginning. As we sat happily at Yaya's luncheon table of a Sunday early in our married life, eating the traditional avgholemono soup, she would announce suddenly, in Greek, "THE ONLY TRUE CHURCH IS THE ORTHODOX CHURCH."

I would say "Uh-huh, yeah, that's certainly true," and Larry, having not understood the Greek and still not one for talking at table, would simply keep on guzzling soup and reaching for another slice of chicken.

"THOSE WHO ARE NOT ORTHODOX WILL NOT SEE HEAVEN!"

"Uh-huh, well . . . ."

Never one to rise to an occasion with the proper squelch, I only thought later of suggesting that some of the family's dearest friends, Baptists, would certainly fry in Hell if we followed this line of thinking. But it wasn't Baptists they were after.

"I read the most terrible thing in the Baltimore paper a few years ago," said Aunt Helen, as we cleared the table. "This Catholic convent burned down in Maryland and when they were clearing up all the rubble, they found THOUSANDS AND THOUSANDS of skeletons of dead babies buried underneath the building."

"Good grief!" I cried. "Was it some kind of cemetery?"

She lowered her voice. "Well, those were babies the nuns had had, and they didn't want people to know about it."

"The NUNS had had? When would the nuns have had time to go out and get pregnant all those dozens of times? When would they have done the laundry and cooked dinner and run the convent? Why didn't I read about it in our papers here?"

"Well, I don't know, maybe it WAS in our papers here and you were just out of town."

I tried to suppress a surge of anger that was rising in my voice. "Tell me approximately when you read it," I said evenly, "and I'll write to the Baltimore newspapers and ask them to research the story. I'd really like to know more about this."

She turned pink and I knew her heart wasn't in it. "Well, it was a long time ago. I don't remember the exact newspaper."

"Maybe it was just some silly anti-Catholic nonsense," I muttered.

Years later, I look back on these incidents and am appalled at my lack of gumption and integrity. Why on EARTH, I ask myself now, did I not stand up for my husband's religion and for common sense in general by saying, "I don't want to hear any more of these foolish old wives' tales in this house. If everyone can't be more open-minded, we won't come here for lunch any more." But, in the manner of the wimpy Greek daughter, I said nothing.

About five years later, Larry told me one day that he had decided to convert to my church. Obstinately, I tried to dissuade him. "I LIKE your church," I said. "It's interesting to go to two churches." I think I was trying to get back at the intolerance through passive resistance.

"Maybe it's interesting," he said, "but your family will be happier if I'm Orthodox. Besides, it will confuse the children if we go back and forth to different churches."

Practically speaking, he was probably right. But I still wish we could have set an ecumenical example.

I am not by any means the only example of a cowed generation, particularly in a household ruled by Mediterranean elders. Among my friends and distant cousins are dozens who have suffered in silence through the Holiday Dinner Syndrome. The law had been laid down early in Yaya's house: all holiday dinners would be there. She preferred not to celebrate a major holiday at someone else's table, even if it were in the home of one of her own flesh and blood.

This led to an entire married life of bitter dispute between my parents at holiday time. "For once in my life," my father would intone angrily, "I would like to have a Christmas dinner in my own house! If they won't come here, we'll eat alone!"

My mother, foreseeing the months of tension and coolness that would follow such a major break in tradition, would cajole and beg and look for reasons why we must all go to her mother's. And in the end we went. I, an innocent child, thought it great fun to go to Yaya's and sit around the big table. I thought Daddy was being difficult, moody and unfair.

And then Larry and I bought our own home in 1970. Yaya had died five years before, but family meals were still around her big table, organized faithfully by the aunts and uncles. On New Year's Day, 1971, Larry announced, "This is the first year I have ever begun in my own home. I never thought I would survive the war to have my own home and family. Why can't we have New Year's dinner here? Surely the family will agree to come here."

A tense, tearful, and bitter campaign began. There were dozens of phone calls, emotional visits to our home by go-betweens. Finally I conceded defeat. I told Larry that, for general peace of mind, we simply must go to the uncles' and aunts' house for New Year's Day. "We can have a wonderful brunch here!" I said.

"I want DINNER here," he responded.

How many thousands of families across the world, Greek or not, have been through this identical dispute? How incredibly silly and pointless it is! And how did we solve the dilemma? Larry solved it in a time-honored Russian way. Early in the afternoon he drank an appreciable number of shots of good Russian vodka. At 5:30 P.M. he smiled at me good-naturedly and said, "Looksh like I'm too drunk to go to the family's housh." And up he went to bed.

And here comes the ultimate example of the cowed generation's reaction. Did I call the family and tell them we had decided to stay in our own home, thereby creating the much-needed break in a strangulating tradition? Heavens, no, I left him home asleep, took the children, and went to the relatives' house, lying and saying Larry had a cold. It took me years before I would admit this act of cowardice to any friends, since I feared they would lecture me for my lack of courage and loyalty to my husband. At last I confessed it to a distant cousin. Nodding morosely, she said, "Yeah. I would have done the exact same thing."

It was, alas, years before we had holiday dinners in our own home, and this finally happened only because many beloved relatives died. But one learns important lessons from these traumas. My mother did. When she was widowed, she moved to the beach cottage two hours away, and one of her first official pronouncements to us was that we did not, repeat DID NOT, have to come to her for holiday meals, nor was she determined to come to ours. "If you want to," she said, "come down with the kids the day after Christmas and we'll have a second celebration here."

We did this for years and, in its way, it too became a happy tradition—Day After Christmas at the Cottage.

Larry and I, as parents now of young people living and working all over the world, have had to remind ourselves not to press them selfishly to be home for specific holidays. There is no less love among us or fondness for tradition if we celebrate events at separate tables. But it was a lesson hard-learned over many, many years.

14
COURTSHIP POSTSCRIPT

After we had been married a few years, I asked Larry one day why he had been so difficult during our courtship. He told me the truth. "I was scared to death. I had been single forty years."

And of course it was true. Who would not fear such a major step? How could he pretend that everything was fun and romantic and normal when, in fact, he was facing a major decision in his life, a change in direction and lifestyle from which—in Larry's opinion to this day—there is no turning back? A decision not to be taken lightly.

After we were married, to my astonishment Larry suddenly began to act romantic, the way the movies and magazines tell you to behave. Since we had been married on a Thursday, Thanksgiving Day, he would bring me six red roses every Thursday as a small anniversary token. This went on for many months, delighting and enrapturing the women at the neighborhood florist shop.

I told him, "This is romantic! Why didn't you do things like this BEFORE we got married?"

"Because," he explained, "you might change your mind and say no, and then I would waste all that money." But in fact he felt seriously that romance and affection are more properly employed in marriage, not in a courtship which is still unofficial. It is a valid and charming idea, generally not subscribed to widely enough.

Looking back on the months in which I knew Larry as a professor but not as a prospective husband, I see now the clues that may, subconsciously, have induced me to accept a marriage proposal from a man who was afraid to follow traditional rules of courtship. One would surely be the afternoon, not long after I began studying Russian, that he invited the Russian and German classes over for tea.

We crowded into his little furnished apartment and saw that he had borrowed a big brass samovar which he had set in the middle of the dining-room table. Around it were thirty cups and saucers that he had rented from United Rent-All. There was one teaspoon on the table. He said, "I forgot to rent spoons. I have one spoon of my own. Everybody use it, and please don't lick it."

As we took turns using the spoon and not licking it, I happened to glance over at his homemade bookshelves—planks and bricks—along the dining-room wall. There, on one plank, was an entire brand new set of the Encyclopedia Britannica. I said to him, "That's a beautiful new Britannica! Did you just get it?"

He answered, "I will be paying for this the rest of my life."

I remember thinking that a man with one spoon and the Encyclopedia Britannica was more to my liking than a man with one hundred spoons and no books. This assessment must surely have been in my subconscious mind when I said, "Yes, I'll marry you," after those three aggravating weeks of non-courtship.

Once a former beau, whom we met by chance at a resort after we had been married about ten years, asked me how I had met Larry. I told him the weird story of our proposal and courtship. Unsmiling, the man said to me, "Are you serious? Why on earth did you marry him?"

Stunned at the impertinence of his question, I grasped at the first answer that came into my mind. "Because he always has a quarter for the toll road."

There was a silence. "What?" said Former Beau.

"I mean it, " I said, realizing that up until that moment this had never occurred to me before, but it was true. "Every time we set out for the Virginia Beach toll road, the quarter is already in his pocket. I don't have to worry about it."

He looked at me for a long time and then changed the subject.

The Encyclopedia Britannica and a quarter for the toll. Does anyone really need any better reasons? And perhaps some roses on a Thursday.

15

AGED NEW PARENTS

We had our first two children within two-and-a-half years, figuring that since our combined ages practically equaled the national debt we had better hurry up and help populate the earth before having to go into the delivery room on walkers.

Our first-born we named Penelope, after my mother, and the second girl was Tamara, for Larry's sister—whom he thought had died in the war.

Our girls are seventeen months apart in age, which we found a delight and a blessing. They liked to play together from the day Tamara began to crawl, and at this writing, with both in their late twenties, they still like to play together—shopping and cooking, renting videos, going to the beach cottage together to swim.

Among their toddler games one year was Greek Church. We had taken them occasionally to the Greek Orthodox church in Durham, NC, since we were living at that time in Chapel Hill. They noted the rituals of the Greek church and occasionally produced their own Orthodox Easter procession, Penny draping a tablecloth around her shoulders and chanting "Amen" or "Kangaroo," holding a magazine aloft like an icon while Tamara trotted along behind, clutching a box of Mueller's spaghetti or any other handy artifact. Tamara, among the best-natured and most obliging children ever to have been born, quietly accepted any prop or theatrical direction given to her by ringleader Penny and carried it out to the best of her ability.

When I found that I was expecting a third baby, I wondered at what point this information should be revealed to the two girls. After all, they were both under three years old and not yet terribly interested in reproduction.

After five or six months, we told them that we were going to have another baby in March. They accepted this information with brief nods and went on playing, not having the slightest idea what "March" meant. I waited for the famous question for which every parent prepares by reading books and magazines. They asked nothing. As I heaved like Moby Dick into the ninth month, I wondered why they hadn't yet noticed my change in shape. Finally, I couldn't stand it another minute.

"Girls," I said to them one night, gathering them as close to my body as my stomach would allow. "You know the baby who's coming in March? Well, do you know where it is?"

They shook their heads.

"It's right in here!" I cried, patting my stomach.

They glanced suspiciously at my stomach. Penny then said cheerfully, "Well, I have a doll in my stomach and Tammy has a teddy bear in hers." And they ran off to play, having disposed of what they considered the most colossal put-on in their experience with quick wit and creativity.

When the baby arrived on time, our downstairs neighbor, Mary Lou Gerrish, was on standby. We left for the hospital at 2 A.M. and she came upstairs to sit with the girls. She told us later that, when they woke up, she announced to them, "Your mother had a baby brother!"

Penny asked, "Is it March?"

"Yes."

"Well, that's good. Because Papa said she looked like a basketball."

Apparently they knew more than they let on.

People had always said dire things like "Oh, you'll be sorry, having them close together like that. You'll be worn to a frazzle. You'll never get out of diapers." This last was partly true, because our son, Nicolai, was born about twenty-two months after Tamara and, for a brief time, there were three of them in diapers. Larry and I debated starting to wear them ourselves to see if we could get a good rebate from the diaper service.

Toilet training became an issue to rival the evening network news in importance. It wasn't until Child Number Three that I discovered a surprising solution to this parental bugaboo. It might even have worked for the first two as well, but then you never know with kids. The solution was simple bribery.

Nicolai wanted a gun. I resisted this desperately, disliking guns intensely in general and finding no redeeming social value in them. I know the familiar argument that pipes and knives and cars kill too, but then they were invented for other reasons—carrying water, cutting bread, driving.

If they kill, it's inadvertent; guns don't have another reason for existence that I have yet noticed. Nonetheless, my son at age three longed for a gun with an astonishing single-mindedness. And what if we wouldn't buy him a gun? He would pick up a pencil, aim it and roar, "Bang, pow, psshhh, ka-BOM." A box of spaghetti served him well as a submachine gun; a shoe could be a bazooka.

One summer afternoon three months after his third birthday, I tried to persuade him to visit the toilet, using all the usual clever arguments. "You can't go to the little boys' play group if you wear diapers." Bad ploy. He said, "I don' WANNA go to the little boys' play group. I wanna stay home wif you."

"Grown-ups go to the toilet! Don't you want to be grown-up?"

"Naw, I'm little. I'm not gwown-up."

Suddenly a sly little smile crossed his features. "Mama! If you buy me a gun, I'll go to the toilet."

I couldn't believe we were having such a sophisticated conversation. "You will? You promise?"

"I pwomise."

I rushed to the neighborhood drug store and began looking over their display of toy guns. Here were 007 Death Kits, Instant Murder Assault Weapons, Fun Flesh-Destroyers. As I put down one terrifying-looking rifle, a neighbor saw me and said, shaking her head, "Isn't it just awful, the scary things they expect our children to play with?"

"It certainly is!" I tsked, and I hurried quickly over to browse at another display, realizing nervously a moment later that I had chosen the condom rack. When I saw that she had left the store, I hurried over and picked up a 49-cent green plastic squirt gun, paid for it and rushed home. Nicolai wasn't put off by my choice of such an innocuous weapon. A deal was a deal. He grabbed the little squirt gun, cradled it possessively to his chest and went straight like an arrow up to the toilet. He never wore diapers again—except at night, because I wasn't THAT trusting. At one point, I said to him plaintively, "Now Nicolai, remember as you play with this that guns are BAD. They kill people."

"Mama," he said with long-suffering patience, "this isn't a REAL gun. This is just a little toy," which of course wrapped up the matter succinctly and taught me not to be so neurotic.

Because the women's movement was just beginning, I became immensely unpopular in those days by saying in public and later in print, in my newspaper column, that these simple days revolving around three small people were the happiest ones of my life. I still think they were, in the light of ultra-sophisticated adventures since then. But part of it may have been due to the fact that our lives were simpler in every respect: we didn't have a house yet and we owned only one car.

These early years were spent in Chapel Hill, NC, because Larry had asked me nervously one day, when Penny was an infant, if I thought he should get a Ph.D. Thrilling to the prospect of being Frau Doktor, which Germans called the wives of Ph.Ds in the days when not many women had them themselves, and envisioning a period of time living the carefree student life, I shouted my assent and we sent in applications to graduate schools.

We decided on the University of North Carolina at Chapel Hill, a graduate student's paradise. Soon we were settled in Odom Village, a student compound of brick apartment buildings and playgrounds where there were more children than mosquitoes and one particularly wonderful advantage— nobody had money. This, we reckon now, was the reason we look back on those years with such affection. Everyone was poor, nobody had good job prospects, everyone was under academic pressure or married to somebody who was. This had all the makings of abject misery and constant depression, and yet everyone seemed supremely happy.

That first year, with babies arriving in swift succession—graduate student wives give birth every nine months—we lived on less than we do now in one month. For one thing, we never went anywhere. This led me to a peculiar social gathering one evening in the neighborhood.

I said to Larry, "Honey, why don't we go some place one night?"

"Honey, we went last year to the delivery room."

"No," I wheedled, "a new and different place!"

"Costs MONEY to go out," observed Larry.

"Not if somebody invites us!"

"Nobody is inviting us!" he countered. "And baby sitter costs money too!"

"Suppose only one of us went out?"

Larry was appalled. "Who would invite only one of us to go out?"

Two days later, magically, the answer appeared in our mailbox. Addressed only to me. "You are invited for a Free Facial at Betty Wood's apartment." Knees buckling in anticipation, I showed him the postcard when he returned from class.

He stared in astonishment at the card. "What is Free Facial?"

"Well, lots of women get together and an expert comes from a make-up company," I babbled, "and then she makes up our faces and we look gorgeous..and then there are refreshments! Things like Hawaiian punch and Lorna Doones! Oh, please, can you babysit that night? I've got to go!"

He looked at me warily as though my mind had at last begun its final journey into oblivion.

"Okay, honey, if you really want to go . . . sounds terrible to me. But if you go, don't buy anything." Silly man, I thought, what would I want to buy? I just wanted the cookies.

The day of the free facial dawned still and humid. It was July in Chapel Hill and 102 degrees. Ole Betty had no air-conditioner. Nonetheless a dozen of us assembled around her dining-room table. She had closed all the windows and drawn the shades, apparently hoping to capture pockets of cool air that might still be in the building since spring. With one bulb in the dining-room fixture bathing us in forty watts of illumination, the room resembled a Turkish bath with a maplewood sideboard and doilies.

And we were ugly. If you know you're going to get a free facial, you make no effort to be stunningly attractive beforehand. We sat around the table, sweating like sows, hoping for Hawaiian punch. Betty served nothing; this wasn't part of the make-up company's package deal.

I whispered to the woman next to me, "Where's the make-up expert?"

"She's in the bedroom getting her equipment together."

It may be an old-fashioned concept, but I expect a make-up expert to resemble someone like the legendary Arlene Francis of TV show fame, or perhaps Rosalind Russell or Irene Dunne. I thought she might have on a hostess gown and would sweep into the room and, baring her teeth under a nicely made-up mouth, say in a theatrical baritone, "Hello, darlings...I'm here to make you stunning!"

Instead the bedroom door opened and a small, thin blonde teenager appeared, her face pale and untouched by creams. She stood by the table and recited her memorized spiel in a Carolina monotone: "How dew yew dew. Ah am here to give yew a free facial." She even emphasized the words "am" and "a" the way airline attendants do when they make the seat-belt announcements.

I was sitting near her and she turned to me first. Picking up a wad of cotton, she rubbed it across my forehead. "Yew are oily-complected!" she said in a tone of reprimand. "Yew need a dark base."

"No, honey, no," I countered, "don't give me a dark base! Don't make me any swarthier than I already am! I want to come out of here looking like a Norwegian."

"Nuh-UH," she said, and she went to work on me. When she had finished, I looked like The Godfather.

We sat through eleven more with no punch or Doones, and then came the fatal concluding statement. "If we sell over $50 of cosmetics tonight, your hostess will get a free kit."

We all turned and stared at the hostess. "I could use that kit," she muttered bitterly. And so I reached for the product list to try to find the cheapest item. It was Astringent Foot-Tightening Lotion. While it did, in fact, make my feet FEEL tight, I still wore the same damned nine-and-a-half mediums a month later. By now it's a ten, but I can borrow my daughters' shoes. Gigantism runs in the family.

Having come late to parenthood, Larry and I acted more like grandparents than parents. While our neighbors by now were used to muttering threats and denials to their children in bored monotones, we bowed and dipped and grinned like aged puppets around the kids, crying "Oh, isn't she DARling?" when one of them knocked over a tin of flour. "She looks just like a little snow-woman!"

Also, we weren't yet adept at lying. It took us a while, innocents that we were, to realize that childhood lying has nothing to do with the behavior of children; it's their parents who lie.

"Man, I'm beat," I would groan at the playground. "Penny hasn't slept for more than one hour straight since she was born. I'm going to be dead before my time."

"Well, she takes a nap, doesn't she?" some other mother would sniff. "What time do you put her down?"

"Put her down?" Maybe that's where I was making my mistake; maybe I was supposed to put her down BANG into the crib with such force that she would be dazed into unconsciousness for a while.

"I put Tinker down at noon," Perfect Mother went on, "and he sleeps till four. Then he plays a little bit and has his supper and his bath and he's down again at seven. Sleeps right through the night."

My jaw hung open. "Down again at seven?" Other mothers nodded in agreement. One added, "You've got to let 'em know who's boss."

The next afternoon, still unsuccessful, I called a neighbor right after lunch to see if I might stop by on my way to the playground with my insomniac daughters. "Come right on," she said, "I just put mine down. Your girls can play on the porch if they're quiet."

As she served me a cup of tea at 1 P.M., I heard screams and blows coming from the nursery. She went in, made a few vicious remarks, and returned to the living room. "They'll settle down soon."

At 1:30, I heard the little sleepyheads moving the beds and bureaus around. "They'll quiet down soon," their mother whispered.

By 2:15, one of the nappers, apparently sleepwalking, was pulling down the window shade as far as it would go and then releasing it so it would shoot up, going whippppppp. My friend shifted uneasily in her seat. I was embarrassed for her and got up to leave, but clearly the situation had not in the least altered her self-image. As I collected my daughters from the porch, she admonished,"You've got to try getting them down for a nap. If they don't get their rest, they'll be unmanageable before long."

16
BECOMING MIHALAP

When our daughter Tamara was an infant, Larry and I had an extremely profound discussion. "You're a Russian and I'm a Greek," I told him. "How can we justify naming our children 'McReed'?"

We decided to take back his real Russian name. This was an interesting and complex matter, involving wedding certificates, social security cards, bank accounts, naturalization papers, and—finally—the two girls' birth certificates. Living as we were in Chapel Hill at the time, we went to the court house in Hillsborough, North Carolina, to change the children's names. A woman in tight white curls and rimless glasses regarded us from behind the counter. "Kin ah hep yew?" she said.

"Yes," I said slowly. "We want to change our children's birth certificates to new names." I was holding Tamara, whom my mother had temporarily nicknamed "Tammy." I nodded toward the baby in my arms. "We want to change this one from Tammy McReed to Tamara Leonidovna Mihalap."

There was a moment of silence and then the woman turned her head to a back door and yelled, "Bill, come in here and HEP me with these people!" They regarded us as certifiably insane.

But the best was yet to come. When our son was born a little over a year later, he came officially into the new name and we printed his birth announcement in the Norfolk paper: "Born March 6, a son, Nicolai Leonidovich Mihalap."

My mother, whose name was Penelope Christopoulos Christopoulos, told me in a nervous whisper, "That poor child has a foreign-sounding name."

Once Larry's original name was restored—though we still called him Larry—we had an even more important discussion. "Why don't you try writing to your father?" I asked one night.

"By now, my father is probably dead," said Larry.

"You don't know that," I replied. "Now that you've got your real name back, I think you ought to try writing to him."

"But he might suffer for it politically."

"Your father would be in his eighties now," I said. "If I were your father, I would be happy to go to Siberia tomorrow just to know that you were living."

Larry wrote a cautious letter to his old address. Six weeks later, an envelope arrived from the Soviet Union. In it, in a stepbrother's handwriting, was a reply from his father.

The letter was, naturally, as cautious as Larry's had been. The second round of letters erased all doubt. With reference to family memories and phrases, each knew that the other was really the real one. From his father's second letter, we learned that Larry's mother, thought to have been killed in battle, had come back from the war to find her husband remarried. But divorce had been contemplated even before the war and soon, officially single again, she too remarried. It was found, too, that the one sister for whom our baby was named, Tamara, was also alive and well.

A rich and emotional correspondence developed, to some extent restricted and then all but terminated by the political climate. Visits were talked about but never accomplished. It was not until 1986 when our oldest daughter Penny took a college semester in Moscow that a meeting could take place. To our sorrow we learned that the grandparents had both died the previous year, but Penny was able to meet her Aunt Tamara and her first cousins. Our nephew Leonid and his wife have since been to the United States to visit us—we who were McReeds!

On a far less significant personal note, we had other international experiences in Chapel Hill. There were a large number of foreign students in the graduate school and we American wives decided to take the initiative in helping the wives learn English. We organized Monday morning coffees in honor of these wives, where we would converse with them in slow and patient English.

After a time, one of the women was able to suggest that the foreign wives sometimes bring refreshments to the coffee. The first to volunteer was Mrs. Moonekorn of Thailand. We Americans tend to think mistakenly that all foreigners are good cooks. Alas, the dishes brought next Monday by Mrs. Moonekorn took some getting used to.

The first was a plate of chips resembling Fritos. We asked what they were and Mrs. Moonekorn, in extremely halting English, replied, "Make from *ko fro*." After some more questions, we realized that *ko fro* , in her Asian pronouncation, was "corn flour." So she had made these corn chips herself! Pleased, we turned to the next dish, which resembled fried rubber bands. Mrs. Moonekorn explained, "Take sweet potato. Glate. Fly." Soon we understood that these were grated, fried sweet potatoes. Something may have gone a little wrong in the process but the intentions were excellent. And then we turned to the third dish, a slightly stale but not unpleasant yellow cake. "This celery cake," said Mrs. Moonekorn. We were amazed.

"You're sure you don't mean carrot cake?" someone asked.

"No," she shook her head. "Make from celery."

"Did you use a blender?" I asked. "How did you mash the celery?"

Her English was not equal to an explanation, so we simply ate it with murmurs of approval as she beamed. We wondered how we would get the recipe. About a month later, a neighbor called. "I found out about Mrs. Moonekorn's celery cake," she said. "It wasn't celery, it was Sara Lee." How could I have missed this, I who had seen with my own eyes at the Metropolitan Opera a check to the box office from the Japanese Consulate made out to "Metloporitan Opela." How uninteresting life would be had there been no Tower of Babel.

When we returned to Norfolk from graduate years in Chapel Hill, it did not take long to realize that we had left the sheltering cocoon of Odom Village and graduated to the real world. We had to have a house now, preferably near Larry's employer,

Old Dominion University. While living horrendously in a spare room at my parents' home, we began to house-hunt, not telling the realtor that our assets at that moment totaled a car, a washing machine, and $35 in cash.

Finally we saw a pleasant white house in an older neighborhood. It had a very pretty long staircase, down which Larry told me he could envision brides descending, and high ceilings. I heard Larry tell the realtor, "We'll take this."

"Wait a minute!" I whispered fiercely, pulling him aside. "We only have $35! This house costs $29,000."

"Well, we borrow the money," he said. "Everybody else does."

Sitting at a desk at the mortgage company, we announced that we wanted to borrow the entire amount on Larry's V.A. loan. Larry showed them his contract for the coming year at the university. "See, I have a job starting next month," he said. "Naturally, we have no money now because we were living on a graduate stipend. So, by next month we can pay a monthly mortgage."

"But surely you have some money for a down payment!"

"Nope," said Larry. "If we had money, we wouldn't ask for loan."

Baffled, they gave us the loan. Then the rental agent said, "You'll need about $2000 in closing costs."

Larry said, "I don't have $2000 worth of clothes."

I kicked him frantically under the desk.

The agent added, "I never did show you that place that you could get on assumption."

"Why wait till Assumption?" said Larry, the good Catholic. "That's August 15th!"

They pushed us through the sale as quickly as possible, fearing worse, and we moved into our friendly, old house in early November, 1969, after my mother and Larry totally undermined their already shaky relationship by painting the interior together while I babysat the kids and my father at my parents' house. The first night we lived in our own home, did we celebrate our status and feel dramatically mature?

No, we lay in bed frozen with fear, realizing that from now on we would have not only monthly mortgage payments but utilities, repairs, taxes, leaking roofs, insurance, termites, and other hideous expenses. As we began to adjust to these shocking new responsibilities, we found ourselves totally immersed in the family nest, just as we had been in Chapel Hill, because none of our old crowd in Norfolk knew we were back in town yet. As Larry had pointed out in that old conversation back before I went to the Free Facial, nobody was inviting us.

And then came the invitation of our dreams. An interior decorator about whom I had once written a newspaper story heard we were back from graduate school and telephoned. "SWEETie," he crooned, "we didn't NAOW you were back in TOWN! Listen, we're having a gourmet club dinner Wednesday night. This is short notice, but can you and Larry possibly join us? It's at Angie's house, black tie, long gown, eight-course French meal with vintage wines. You would be our guests, of course. Can you come?"

"Can we come?" I croaked. "We'll crawl over broken glass."

The night of the gourmet dinner approached. The children hadn't seen a baby-sitter in over a year. We called my mother, but for once she couldn't make it. We hired a neighbor's teen-aged daughter for the evening but were afraid to tell this to the children, even though we were bigger than they were.

As we dressed for the grand occasion the children came to our bedroom and stood around in a little semi-circle, watching a phenomenon of a caliber they had never before witnessed. As Larry began to shave and I fastened dangling earrings to my ear lobes, Penny asked the first question in a sinister crescendo: "Where you gonNA GO?"

"Well, we're just going to run down the street for a few minutes to see some people . . . ."

Before I could finish the lie, they began to cry in unison, a hideous cry that started softly and then, like a siren picking up volume as it neared the scene of the accident, erupting into a caterwauling that shook the window panes. A police cruiser slowed down outside the house, alerted no doubt by some obnoxious eavesdropping neighbor.

"Who's gonna stay wif us?" came out, between strangled sobs.

"This nice girl, you'll just love her.."

This was the signal for them to begin gagging and turning blue. Larry had long since cut himself five times shaving and slapped half a roll of toilet paper over his face. I knocked over a bottle of Joy perfume I had been hoarding for seven years.

We started down the steps to answer the doorbell, and the children purposely fell head over heels down the stairs, attempting suicide—a startlingly sophisticated concept for persons under the age of five. The babysitter was admitted, and Nicolai threw up at once.

Realizing suddenly that I had it in my power to distract them with humor, a tool I had already used successfully many times, I squatted down alongside their flailing bodies. "Kids, listen to me, LISTEN to me. Wait'll you hear THIS! You know that house where we're going? I'm going to call you up from there!"

"I don't care!" gagged Tamara, while Nicolai bit the baby-sitter's ankle.

"Wait, I'm not finished yet! I'm going to call you up and. . ." I paused and made a grotesque face, "talk SPOOKY on the phone."

They were suddenly silent. "How you gonna talk spooky on the phone?"

"I can't do it here!" I leered, eyes narrowed, "I can only do it over the phone. You just WAIT till you hear it!"

And as they mulled this information over between shaky breaths, Larry and I dashed out of the house, leapt into the car and drove in reverse for two blocks. We then set off down the expressway to Virginia Beach, where Angie's elegant home was located. For twenty-three miles, not one word passed between us. Our first night out together in four years . . . . And then, as we turned into the driveway of the gourmet dinner, he turned to me and, no doubt moved suddenly by the romance of the occasion, yelled, "Do you think the children are all right?"

"Well, dammit, how do I know?" I screamed back. We entered the baronial entrance hall of the house, to find waiters standing by the door with trays of rare champagne. I accepted a glass and whispered, "Where is your telephone, please?"

"In this room, madam," said the butler, showing me to an exquisite little library full of beautiful paintings and rare antiques. One other guest was sitting in there sipping a glass of Dubonnet. She was a cultural leader of the area, a woman I had heard of, and she was exquisitely gowned and wearing long diamond earrings. She nodded politely: "Good evening."

"Well, HI!" I effused, swaying my jaw a little in what I felt was an aristocratic manner. I picked up the phone and dialed home.

It was Penny who answered, not the baby sitter. "Baby," I murmured *sotto voce*, "this is Mummy."

She said, "Talk spooky."

I looked over at the cultural leader, who was examining a painting with her eyes half-shut, while sipping her wine. I thought, she's not paying attention to me anyway. Turning back to the phone, I gave my world champion Dracula laugh: "Moo-hoo-hoo-ha-ha-HA-HAAAAA!"

The cultural leader spat half the glass of Dubonnet into an oil painting and then had a coughing fit that lasted approximately seven minutes. She looked at me oddly and walked in silence to the bathroom. At dinner, I was seated next to her.

Both Larry and I had indigestion, and it wasn't the tournedos Rossini. It was the sure knowledge that our life style had suddenly changed irrevocably. As yet we hadn't realized that it was probably for the better.

In our early years as parents, we discovered that one of our greatest obstacles to enjoyment of this job, along with all those lies the other parents kept telling, was gratuitous advice.

"Do you let her eat that? I wouldn't, if I were you. They get into bad habits real fast."

"You've got to let her know who's boss. If she won't sleep, give her something to make her sleep." (A mickey?) "She's three weeks old now, she ought to be on your schedule."

Sometimes, of course, we brought the advice on ourselves. I still do, even when it no longer concerns my children. It is the mark of the natural comedienne to make fun of herself; this is the source of most of my humor. Many mistake this self-deprecation, not unnaturally, for insecurity and feel compelled at once, from their vantage points of maturity and success, to give advice. On the contrary, if I wanted advice I would probably ask for it. Probably. All I really want is a laugh.

And so when I groaned that our nightly ritual of dramatic and original bedtime stories, lasting one or two hours, was wearing me out, I would inevitably hear, "Tell them Mommy doesn't feel like telling a story tonight. Make them invent their own stories; you're not their slave." But some hidden feeling—or perhaps the vague memory of being told hours of wonderful stories by my own exhausted parents, stories that laid the groundwork in my own mind for a certain creative craziness—kept me telling and then wondering if I had been wrong not to heed what the experts thought to be brilliant advice.

Funny how one never considers the source of advice. Does one really want to be like the adviser? That being the crux of it all, I wonder why we didn't stop to think of that right away when Jean, our new next door neighbor in Norfolk, began dropping hints like, "Boy, I'm certainly glad I had that hysterectomy. No more worries about pregnancy for ME."

"Yes, that's wonderful," I said absently, wondering why she was worried about pregnancy when it seemed she ought to be long past menopause.

A few minutes later: "I sure hope you and Larry aren't thinking of having more children. This world's too full of children as it is. Maybe you ought to have a hysterectomy." Then, approaching the real core of the problem, "You know, you two give those children too much attention. They're going to come between you. You need time to yourselves."

As I nodded politely and told her I'd certainly keep that in mind, I wondered what she had seen the kids do that made her think Larry and I were ready to take out contracts on one another. And then the *coup de grace*: "You-all don't beat those children enough. We've never seen either one of you take a strap to them. You need to give them a really good whipping now and then. Children appreciate it."

The hell of it was, her adolescent children were polite and well-behaved. Could she, horribly, be right? We sat at night, worrying and discussing it, wondering if the neighborhood civic league had had a meeting to discuss the fact that we were not beating our children the way we should.

It was not until the fateful dining-room episode that I suddenly understood how to deal with Jean's advice. She came over for coffee and, as the kids greeted her at the door shouting happily, "Mama, look who's here!", she shook her head in resignation, tsked a few times, and then said to me when they were out of earshot, "You let them make too much noise when people come into the house. When my children were three and four years old, if a grown-up came in the house, you know what they did? They went over and sat on the couch and lowered their heads and DID NOT LOOK UP until I told them they could."

I recalled a movie I had seen once of a Roman centurion waving a big whip over the oarsmen on a galley ship. She continued, "And you let them stay up too late. We can look right out our living-room windows and see them running around your dining-room late at night. Our children used to be in bed at six o'clock every single night until they started school."

I pondered Jean's words all afternoon. Should I finally buy a whip? If we got big leather straps and secured the children to the beds at night right after supper, would we in fact enjoy our own tuna-fish casseroles more and Find Romance? What about daylight savings time, ought we to get them eyepatches at night to fool them?

And then, that night, it occurred to me that I had lost my sense of humor. I also wondered suddenly if the kids still had theirs. I said to Penny and Tamara, ages five and four, "Listen, kids, when you're playing in the dining-room after supper, do me a favor. Whenever you get near the big windows, the ones next to the neighbors' house, ask me what time it is. If it's after 6:30, I want you to fall down on your stomachs and crawl under the window so the neighbors can't see you."

"Oh, boy! Why, Mama?"

"Because they get mad if children stay up after 6:30, so we don't want to make them mad. Let them just be happy, thinking you're in bed."

They understood! That night they screeched to a stop in front of the big window. "What time is it, Mama?"

"Eight o'clock."

"Is that after 6:30?"

"Yeah! You know what to do!"

Wham! Down on their stomachs they went, crawling like GIs under barbed wire, giggling joyously. Jean never said anything else. I think we fooled her. We also finally bought curtains.

If the kids caught on to our satisfaction to these witty little intrigues, it might have been because they were probably smarter than we were. When I took Penny for her well-baby check-up at age three, the pediatrician said, "Let's check her hearing." He put a huge pair of earphones on her head and said, "Tell me what you hear, Penny!"

She crossed her eyes and said, "Guh-guh-guh-guh-guh."

"Is that what she's supposed to hear?" I asked nervously.

"Uh, no," he said. "Is she at all verbal?"

"Is she VERBAL?" I cried. "My God, she's been reciting dirty Greek poems since she was a baby."

"Uh-huh," he said. "Well, let's just forget the hearing test and look at her coordination." He set her down on the floor, crossed the room and held out his arms. "Walk across the room to me, Penny."

The kid fell on her stomach and flailed in place like a seal.

"Come on, Penny, WALK!" I snapped.

"Don't upset her," he cautioned. "Sometimes they're a little slow learning muscular control."

"SLOW?! She was <u>running</u> at eight months!"

When we got out to the doctor's parking lot, I began strapping her into her infant seat. She turned to me and said, "Why didn't he give me a DPT booster?"

In retrospect, then, should we have taken more advice, paid greater attention to the baby books and followed more rules? Well, maybe so— but the kids, now in their twenties, are funny, compassionate and intelligent. They like good food, they're tolerant, they can take care of themselves and they love us and each other, even when our ideas of social proprieties remain in the dark ages, impervious to change. Is there anything else we should want? Of course we have friends who think we should have pushed them into more traditional or lucrative careers,

The kids, with their customary grins, in the late 1980's. Left to right: Tamara, Nicolai, Penny.

since, after careful thought, they have all decided to be either starving artists or starving teachers. But life is short and success relative. And consider their peculiar parental role models, after all.

Financial worries, such as they were, were a prime topic of conversation in the early days of our marriage, to the extent that we learned belatedly an important fact: if you talk too much about something worrisome in front of alert children, this concern can become part of their psyche for eternity. Our daughter Penny overheard so much during babyhood about bills and mortgages that she is now without question the world's most fiercely economical human being, to the point that less thrifty members of the family, her parents included, get into wrangles with her.

I asked our second daughter, Tamara, why she and her brother do not share this trait with Penny, and she pointed out thoughtfully that Penny's mind was perhaps more of a steel trap in those formative years than is usually the case. "Everything you harped on," she opined, "went into her brain and stayed there. That's why she likes food so much, too."

In fact all of us like food, but Penny eats more heartily, shows more interest in it and oddly enough stays thinner than any of the rest of us. This is the combined fault of both her parents who, in true old world fashion, plied our tiny children with morsels and harangued them at all times to eat second helpings. Penny told us that she had never met anyone who didn't eat a second helping until she went to college where, to her astonishment, classmates would push their plates away, satisfied, after half a dinner.

"I even took second helpings of the gross stuff," she confessed, recalling what lengths she would go to in the dormitory to make the institutional food palatable, putting slices of cheese on top of broccoli and microwaving it, then seasoning heavily with pepper or a little oil and lemon. Observers would gag and point, just as friends did when I followed the same pattern in my own college dorm, seasoning vile pot roast lightly with vinegar and a pinch of sugar in an attempt to create sauerbraten.

Our preoccupation with low income was a factor in a decision early in our marriage regarding Christmas presents. Larry and I concluded that it was foolish to give one another gifts when our joint bank account was so ridiculously low. We agreed to limit presents at Christmas to things for the children. Our own gift, we knew, would be the pleasure derived from watching them open the packages. As years have gone by, we have abandoned this plan, but now all of us, including the kids, agree that there are too many boxes under the tree and that Christmas was better when things were fewer and, hence, more appreciated.

However, in those early years we stuck to the rules, until the day soon after our purchase of the Norfolk house when I was skimming through *Opera News* magazine and spotted a review of a new recording—Tchaikovsky's *Eugene Onegin*, performed by the Bolshoi Opera. Now this was a major milestone for the Mihalap family.

While I had been involved in opera for years, Larry had never seen or heard one until we were married. Nevertheless, like all young Russians he had not only studied Pushkin's immortal poem/novel *Eugene Onegin* in school but had memorized and adored it. It was his dream to hear the Tchaikovsky opera based on the poem. Early in our marriage we spotted the only available recording, done by a Yugoslavian opera company, and we bought it regardless of cost.

After listening to the first three minutes of the recording, Larry yelled, "Demmit! They do not palatalize their consonants!"

I wasn't as distracted by these little pronunciation problems as he was, but his disgust was contagious, and soon we stopped listening to the Belgrade singers and put the records away. Now, at last, there was a new recording done by the ultimate Russian performing group. I went downtown to the music store and ordered the Bolshoi *Eugene Onegin*.

After some three weeks, in late November, they called to tell me the records had come in, giving the opera's name a charmingly American pronunciation: "Your Eugene One Gin is here." I picked up the package, brought it home, and hid it.

The next afternoon Larry, who usually walked the mile and a half from campus, called from his office. "Honey, can you pick me up today? I have too many books to carry."

When he climbed into the car at the university he was holding a large, square box. "Just some big new book I ordered from the Russian book company," he muttered nervously.

I fixed my eyes on his face. "No , it isn't. It's the new Bolshoi recording of *Eugene Onegin.* "

He was stunned. "How did you know?"

"Because I just bought it for you."

That Christmas morning, for the first time since the babies were born, there were two packages under the tree for Mama and Papa. They contained the same thing, but we kept them both. O. Henry would have liked it.

17
CLIMBING ONTO
THE PLATFORM

While it was, of course, a delight for the children to have a whole big house to play in, Larry and I were not natural home-owners. Owning a house terrified us. There were things to repair, horrifying expenses never anticipated in advance, rooms that had to be Done. I never knew how to do anything, relying without question on anything my house-oriented mother suggested or did for us without suggesting. This angered Larry, who felt she interfered; I countered that she wasn't interfering because I had no ideas of my own for her to interfere with.

Better yet, we never bought anything for the house. My parents sent over by moving van all the excess furniture and rugs, china and antiques from their house. Over the years, like anyone who grew up in the Depression and then could finally afford to buy things, they had accumulated enough stuff for ten houses, and it was beginning to panic my mother. When, later, she and my father sold their house and moved to their beach cottage, a moving van brought over everything we hadn't taken the first time. We filled the house, the garage, the cellar, and an attic. Now I felt panicked. And still do. I live in dread that my three children will want to buy their own things. Every night I pray, "Oh, let them be hippies, let them be hippies!" so that they won't own anything decent and I can foist everything over on them before I reach my dotage.

By now I have finally grown up enough to buy a curtain on my own, but probably there is in me some deep-seated wanderlust that rejects the permanent nest—at least on a constant basis—because I have happily pursued a career that takes me out of town fairly frequently and hurls me into motel rooms. Do I weary of these ordinary-looking motel rooms with their large, private television sets, room service, and stacks of towels? Don't be ridiculous.

And there is the added attraction of the audience. Ah, the ham's affection for a sea of faces, the lifting of the heart at a burst of laughter! I contemplate with amazement all my friends who break out into cold sweats when they have to give treasurer's reports before ten women, yet were not ill at ease walking down long church aisles while platoons of bridesmaids and six hundred people turned to watch every step! Ye gods, think of the potential for disaster THERE—a heel caught in the train, a ring leaping out of the bridegroom's grip and plummeting through a heating register, ushers fainting and candles falling over and igniting the priest's robes! All I have to worry about is a squealing microphone and maybe an occasional spinach leaf caught between my teeth.

Almost everybody speaks in public once in a while, so it's peculiar to think of it as a profession. Let's face it: maybe it isn't the average profession. In most cases people are hired to speak because they are already expert enough to be paid for doing something else. This is why it's difficult for professional speakers to explain why they need to be paid just for speaking. It seems inconceivable that they don't have some other source of income. What, THIS is what you do for a living?

But if you do it in such a way that it begins to become entertainment or education, then we're looking at a possible reason. The summer before I was married, my parents invited a group of friends to their house for dinner. As always, the family took advantage of my affinity for vivid anecdote as a little after-dinner entertainment. My mother said, "Hope, tell everybody about those women you heard fighting in the bank in New York!"

This incident was actually not such a bad story. I assumed the character of a tough, heavy girl behind me in line, a girl with a tall, black bee-hive hairdo and lots of mascara. She kept saying, "It should never fail I always get this lousy woman teller. If I got the other teller, I woulda been outa here by now, back at my dest drinkin' coffee. It should never fail."

When the sour-faced woman in front of me turned and looked at Mascara, the tough broad snapped, "You want something, Miss? You want something, that you're lookin' at me like that?"

And the second woman responded, "Lady, I'm warnin' yez. If you start wit me you're startin' wit the wrong person."

This poignant story was only the beginning that evening. It would have taken a gag or a tranquilizer to shut me up after that. I went on to the New York girdle saleswoman to the Virginia teenagers to the girl from a Greenwich Village Academy of Deeper Thought doing her master's thesis in modern dance.

One of the guests, the curator of the Norfolk Museum, drew me aside as the guests were leaving. "Can you do a full evening of this sort of thing for our museum membership next month?"

"WHAT?" I gasped. "How long is a full evening?"

"Oh, 8:00 to 10:00," he said cheerfully, "with maybe a little intermission. It's our annual wine-and-cheese cabaret and I think this would be marvelously different entertainment."

Boy, you're not kidding, I thought. "Oh, Brian," I mumbled, "I don't see how I could come up with that much funny stuff."

He then said some unexpected magic words: "We'll pay you."

It was the first time anyone had ever offered to pay me for being funny. I told him I would call him the next day, and that night I sat down to discuss this amazing offer with my mother. "Oh, well, of course you can do that!" she said. (What can I tell you, she was my mother.) "There are tons of funny things you could do."

"Name some," I groaned.

And she did, naming things I had said in passing for years, little bits and pieces of funny observation and anecdote that I had never in a million years thought might be suitable for an audience of strangers. "Do you think they'd laugh at THAT?" "Of course they would, it's funny."

By the time the dreaded one-woman show rolled around on August 11, 1964, I had more than two hours of material—from anecdotes about the opera to impressions of every imaginable type of American and foreigner—including several knock-out new things invented for the occasion with the excellent kibitzing of a parent who, though she herself could not perform, knew what would be appealing to an audience. She was a born director—which, I assure you, many performers, myself included, are not.

Once you've done a show, the word spreads. Soon another group asked for a similar one-woman show, then another. The great breakthrough came several years later when an organization called one morning in desperation to see if I were free that very evening. "We were bringing in some national speaker from out of town," the program chairman explained, "and he got sick. The speakers' bureau can't find a replacement on such short notice. I heard you last year at the Rotary Club—could you come out and do your program for us?"

It was a success, and I learned that this organization brought in out-of-town speakers all the time. They told me I could come to their next banquet to hear the professional humorist who would be appearing. "Aha," I thought, "now I'll see what a real professional does on the platform."

That night the real professional bombed. Hideously. Even as I felt enormous empathy for this well-meaning speaker whose humor had not appealed to the Norfolk audience, I recognized full well that it could happen to anyone, and has. But I made no comment.

Two weeks later I had a call from the speakers' bureau that had provided the unappreciated program. "Well, we hear that the folks in Norfolk liked you better than any of the speakers we've sent them this year. Where can we hear you?"

They offered me a date in a nearby city, and my career began.

On the other hand, as I was musing above, can one really call "speaking" a career? I keep thinking I ought to get a job. Then once I have it I could talk about it and be an expert and, hence, a speaker again. But, actually, humorists <u>are</u> in essence talking about their jobs, albeit in retrospect. In every wild program I present are reminiscences about my jobs as a Greek child in Virginia, as a college student in Poughkeepsie, as a secretary who didn't know shorthand, as a newspaper writer who never studied journalism.

After some concentration and deliberation, you find hidden uplifting messages, as much as you may resist them, behind all the funny stories. And, when you get up enough nerve to mention them—because God forbid the audience should stop laughing for a minute— you find that you have now entered a new and more lucrative category: motivational humor.

In the course of coming up with all this profundity, I began learning my trade and helping pad the family income by traveling all over creation to give after-dinner speeches, particularly at first for the grand old Associated Clubs circuit. There could be no better training-ground for public speaking, for this circuit was founded back in the early forties by the late Benjamin Franklin of Topeka, Kansas, for one purpose only—to create platforms for good speakers, in the tradition of the historic Chautauqua lecturers.

The rules for doing well speaking to Associated Clubs dinners are simple: no off-color material, plenty of humor, if possible a bit of inspirational message, no radical agendas. The audiences, most of them elderly couples or widows, bring one charming attribute to their meetings: they are there, with enthusiasm, <u>to hear a speaker</u>. This is not always the case when one is the featured speaker at a banquet.

Sometimes people are at a banquet to see who gets the awards and to curse about it later. Sometimes the cocktail party beforehand is the bigger draw, and you can tell it all too well, especially when fifteen women get up in a group to go to the ladies' room and walk in front of you as you're speaking, giggling, "Well, I said to him..."..."Come ON, Lucille, you're a slowpoke!"..."I hope you have your lipstick, cuz I changed purses."..."Lord, I hope I make it, I had three of those whiskey sours and my bladder's 'bout to burst!"

The Associated Clubs audiences, subscribers each year to four or five dinners with speakers, arrive at the dinner location as early as 4:30 P.M. to get good seats. They turn their chairs to face you, sit back, fold their hands and smile expectantly as you begin. Speaking of turning chairs around, I have spoken to many an audience in which people, seated at round tables with their backs to the lectern, just stay that way, staring at their empty dessert dishes throughout the whole program as the speakers talk animatedly to their backs. They probably figure it's a breach of etiquette to move their chairs. Makes you think you're speaking from the back of the bus.

But even the best speaking circuit provides eccentric situations. I look back to a period in 1979-80 when I was away for two and a half weeks, speaking in a different city each night. This was possible only because my mother came to stay at our house to be surrogate mother and cook, a circumstance that worked nicely because our methods were alike and the kids adored her. At the end of that tour, feeling guilty nonetheless, I asked the children as I fixed them pancakes one morning, "Really, babies, tell me the truth. Wasn't I away too much this time? I'll never do it again."

As one, they cried out, "No, Mama, it's fun when you go away! You bring us back all those neat presents and write those goofy cards." I still didn't believe them, no matter what they said. It was important to me that I feel a little guilty; guilt is such a comforting, old-world emotion.

Even though Grandmother—or Vaga, as my children called her when they were trying to learn to say the Greek "yaya"— could come to stay while I was away speaking, I still felt that my major role in life was running the household. And I had to make the family feel that I was still doing it in absentia.

Consequently, every time I planned to leave home for a few days on the road speaking, I would make major, comprehensive preparations. I still do to a less extravagant extent, even though the kids are now all out of the nest and my husband is the only one remaining who needs attention.

The chief preparation—inevitably, for one of Greek descent—involved food. My first job, if I expected to be away four or five days, would be to devise menus. I love to make up menus. Cooking is, after all, the one thing I really like to do best at home. You have already read of my lack of initiative in interior decoration and repair. Sewing and cleaning are also low on my list of homely talents. But cooking? What a comfort! What therapy, after dealing with clients and bookings and marketing, the tension of an occasional cool audience, the stress of meeting deadlines.

There sit the friendly ingredients, waiting to be combined into a tasty, soul-satisfying menu, bringing forth praise and smacking of lips from those I love! The ingredients don't talk back; I don't have to sell them anything. There they sit, like the beloved shmoos years ago in the Li'l Abner comic strip, wanting nothing more than to be consumed and enjoyed.

And so a day or two before departing on a whirlwind speaking trip, I would assemble meal plans of all the things the troops like best and then go to the store to buy the ingredients. Where possible, I would cook the morsels and store them in refrigerator or freezer.

Then I would prepare the charts. First there would be one entitled THINGS TO REMEBER.

TUESDAY:	Man coming to check air-conditioner in am
	Larry, dentist at 2:30 pm
	Mail mortgage check

Then came the meals, typed appealingly, menu-style, on eight by ten white paper. For example:

MONDAY: <u>Breakfast</u> English muffins on second shelf refrigerator Honey and blackberry jam in pantry Tiny smoked sausages in meat bin <u>Lunch</u> Make yourself sandwiches for school: turkey breast in meat bin, peaches and apples in fruit bin, good jalapeno cheese! <u>Dinner</u> Meat loaf—3rd shelf of refrig., bake at 350 for 40-45 minutes, uncovered Baked potatoes (put in oven 10-15 minutes ahead of meat loaf) Sour cream and grated cheddar on top refrig. shelf Fresh green beans already cooked; reheat and season with olive oil and lemon juice Long cucumber in crisper for slicing; sprinkle with dill weed and a little salt

Finally, on the third chart, I would type my itinerary—flight numbers and times, hotels with phone numbers, site of the speech, name of client.

Naturally, as the kids have left home many of these instructions have become superfluous—except that Larry still asks hopefully if I am going to leave him a couple of casseroles he can heat up while I'm away. And I do.

Let me now admit that I know full well this Supermom Method has served to keep everyone dependent on me. What I probably should have done way back when the kids were in junior high and perfectly able to take responsibility—to say nothing of Larry, who cooked for himself for years before he married me—was to snap, "All right, everybody. You're on your own. I'm going off to make money, you people make up your own set of menus, do your own shopping and keep house. Take turns, now. Penny, you get Monday and Thursday, Tamara, you get..."

It's too late now. I admit my failure in this respect, and my only defense is the old ethnic background and, simply, selfishness. It's the Mediterranean Mother Syndrome, to say nothing of the fact that, let's face it, I LIKE to make the #*$&!! casseroles and write the charts. It's a masochistic way to feel needed, I grant you, but it works for some of us. And the kids have learned to cook by example anyway, because I can't very well send them casseroles to their work locales: Yemen, China, Portugal, North Carolina and other exotic places.

On my first long speaking trip to the West Coast, I landed at the Seattle-Tacoma airport at one in the morning where, as I awaited the downtown shuttle bus, a bright-faced young girl tried to convert me to her religious movement. She told me proudly that she had left her family and joined a denomination that sent its young members door to door. I told her that I admired her conviction but it embarrassed me when people tried to convert me and that I thought it was wrong and unchristian to upset her family; she pointed out that, according to the Gospels, true faith was as a sword—which she pronounced like "swore" with the "w"sounding—between true believers and their families. I was still embarrassed and now also distracted by the "w."

Before she could continue, the shuttle bus arrived, and I made a dash for it. The driver, learning I was a Virginian, announced that he was from Loo-ziana and, after half an hour, got to be such a bore about it that I offered him the sandwich I had been saving for my hotel room so that he would put it into his mouth and stop talking.

Like any dedicated eater, I spent a good part of my first day in Tacoma—as I do in any new city— ferreting out regional delicacies, such as salmon smoked over alderwood and served with melted butter. Perhaps one reason I don't tire of travel is that eating out in new places appeals to me greatly and is the best part of a day off.

People-watching, a valuable tool for the humorist, became a major event on this trip. A whole new aspect of the wanderer's life was introduced to me the morning after my speech, when I took the airport limo again to head on to Spokane. Joining me in the van were Marie, Helen and Harvey.

The three of them climbed boisterously into the van at 8:30 A.M., bringing with them the scent of early-morning cocktails and tobacco. Marie, a grandmotherly woman with tight grey curls, rimless glasses and a bright pink pants suit asked the driver if she could smoke—he said yes—and then gave a cough that nearly blew the roof off the limo.

Harvey, Helen's young husband, wore a black jacket covered with decorative metal studs and jeans so low-cut that when he leaned forward to say something to the driver, an appreciable amount of bare back and rear end appeared between the jacket and his belt. Helen's rough, lined face was framed by a big, black pompadour and shoulder length hair. Her big grin was not in the least hampered by two missing front teeth.

We stopped at the Greyhound station, Harvey's stop, and he jumped out and ran over to a man with heavy sideburns and a substantial beer belly hanging over his belt. "God bless him; he's found EUgene!" cried Marie. "If that S.O.B. don't come over here and give me a kiss, I'll kick his butt!"

A quiet, bespectacled man sitting behind me, holding a briefcase labeled "Pacific Lutheran University," blinked and looked unsmilingly out of the window.

Marie and Helen kissed the boys goodbye, and we set off. The women lit up and chattered happily about the trip to come, which we soon gleaned was a barmaids' reunion in Spokane. I smiled at one of Marie's jokes and she saw it. Immediately, I was drawn warmly into their conversation, learning that Marie had met Helen working at the Mission Tavern in Dayton,

Washington, when the Jolly Green Giant company had extra workers in town for asparagus season.

"Lots of workers come up from Mexico for that, y'know," she said, "and jeez, them taverns is BUSY. Hey, Helen, remember the night that guy got stabbed in the men's room?"

"Served him right," said Helen.

"Say, let's just get one way tickets to Spokane and take the bus back through Dayton. We'll terrorize the place. Waddaya say, Helen?"

A car swerved close to our limousine and Marie rolled down her window, leaned out, and called, "Up yours, buster!" The Pacific Lutheran professor coughed and closed his eyes.

The women learned to their delight that they and I were to be on the same flight to Spokane. Since there was an hour to spare, they invited me at once into the airport bar and, over Bloody Marys and milk punches, told me about Helen's intestinal by-pass surgery (she had lost 150 pounds) and about ex-husbands who had beaten them.

"Buddy used to tie me to the bedposts with his socks and knock me unconscious!" related Helen, grinning happily at the memory.

"You didn't call the police?"

"Aw, heck no! That's family business."

When we boarded our flight, they headed for the smoking section. I could hear them partying all the way to Spokane. Upon our arrival, a dignified elderly man was waiting for me at the gate. "Mrs. Mihalap?" he boomed in a ministerial voice. "So happy to have you in our fine city!"

A few feet away, Marie and Helen staggered out of the jetway. "Hey, Hope!" Marie yelled, with a wink at my companion. "Don't do nothin' I wouldn't enjoy doin'!"

One thing I learned from the beginning on the Another Opening/Another Town circuit was never to prejudge an audience on the basis of its location. This was, in fact, something I knew already from having given a one-woman show in

Moyock, North Carolina, the first year I started performing. Moyock is a very small town just over the southeastern border of Virginia and its town hall series was held in the high school auditorium. I was afraid my rendition of a Richmond, Virginia, garden clubber doing a book review of *Lady Chatterley's Lover*, though perfectly innocent, might contain some material beyond their frames of reference.

They turned out to be one of the most cosmopolitan audiences I have ever encountered, laughing uproariously not only at the garden clubber but also at my imitation of "Opera News on the Air," which isn't something to which too many audiences can relate.

I was not too surprised, therefore, to discover that the Associated Clubs audience in Yakima, Washington, consisted of simple apple farmers who took frequent vacations to Singapore, Australia, Belgium, and Hong Kong and wanted a speech heavy on opera stories. Or that the farming community audience in Waterloo, Iowa, served Caesar salad and tournedos at its banquet and had just hosted a distinguished Soviet delegation.

One thing that has always caused consternation on these speaking trips is my last name. The poor soul who has to introduce me approaches me in a state of paranoia, ready for an intensive course on how to pronounce Mihalap. It's true, we should probably spell it some other way, but how? Michelob would have been smart, but it's too late now. In Roswell, New Mexico, the elderly program chairman had me come down to the hotel lobby an hour before receiving-line time so that we could work on the pronunciation of my name.

I foolishly tried the correct way first. "Mee-ha-lopp," I said, "sort of like Michelob, only with a foreign accent."

He stared at me confused. "Ay? Sort of like WHAT?" I realized he had not heard of Michelob.

"Well, how about M'hallop," I suggested, "rhyming with gallop."

"I thought it was M'hay-lup," he snorted.

"Well, that would be fine too! Go right ahead and say M'hay-lup!"

That night he stood up and said, first, "This lady comes from Nor-fork, Virginia. Lousiest place I ever went to in my life, back in '43." Then he continued, "Can't figure out what she's going to talk about tonight. I hope she knows." And then, "So, I present to you tonight—Miz Hope Miss-hap."

One thing I learned early on was to tell the program chairman in clear, unmistakable terms that the reason I was leaving the head table was so that I could go to the ladies' room. You have to make things like that very clear, because back in Kings Mountain, North Carolina, I simply got up from my seat, nodded and smiled encouragingly at the program chairman, and went off to the facilities, down a corridor about half a block long.

The building was an old VFW hall and the walls were thin. No sooner was I settled in a ladies' room cubicle when, through the wall, I heard the chairman's voice over the microphone. "Our speaker tonight comes to us from Norfolk, Virginia."

Ye gods, I thought, he's INTRODUCING me. WHY? He had obviously mistaken my friendly nod for a cue. I leapt up from the seat, stockings twisted, and debated frantically over whether or not to flush. If I could hear him, they could probably hear the toilet. With no time to straighten my hair or put on lipstick, I flew maniacally down the hall and burst into the dining room door as he announced, "Hope Miller-snap!"

Larry was with me that night and didn't notice the near trauma. "I just thought you looked little bit nervous," he said.

But it was nowhere near as superb an experience as that of my mother, who went to a dance in 1938 wearing an elegant cocktail dress she had, as always, made herself. It had a big rose at the waist and her shoes had been dyed to match; she was a knockout.

When the band took a break she went to the ladies' room and then, re-entering the hall, walked right down the middle of the big dance floor to her table. All eyes were on her, great smiles wreathed people's faces. "I am," she thought, "the belle of this ball."

When she reached her seat, sat down and crossed her legs, she noticed, impaled on one of her high heels, the end of an entire roll of toilet paper she had trailed with her down the dance hall floor.

I began slowly to branch out from the Associated Clubs circuit as other groups heard of me by word of mouth. Finally a fellow speaker on the circuit suggested I join the National Speakers Association. Why shouldn't we have our union too? And what an advantage, not to have to pay for speakers for our conventions!

Ben Franklin the younger, now head of his father's Associated Clubs circuit, told me it was an excellent idea and he proposed me for membership. So did a fellow speaker and generous mentor, the late Bill Woodruff. Within a couple of years I did a brief program at a convention, and this launched me into a new market. Speakers' bureaus took notice and proposed me for corporate conferences.

From time to time, no matter how adept you become at holding an audience, you hit a bummer. I shall never forget Acapulco. The 350 salesmen in the audience, sunburnt from a day-long fishing trip and punchy from cocktails and roast beef, stared at me with hostility as their 90-year-old president introduced me: "It says here on this piece of paper that this lady is the Greek Erma Bombeck. Well, I don't know who the hell Erma Bombeck is, so this means nothing to me." And he sat down.

I said, "I'm Erma Bombeck and I'm happy to be here tonight," which was a dumb thing to say but it got a great laugh. And then, apparently fearing they had in some way insulted their elderly president, they fixed their faces into masks of distrust and didn't laugh again for fifty minutes. Some of them put their heads down on the tables and closed their eyes, others kept looking at their watches and tapping their feet, a couple of lucky ones sitting near the back sneaked out to smoke.

This confirms my opinion that the riskiest audience in the world is one composed entirely of businessmen. If they have been in meetings all day they probably want to drink, play cards, flirt in the hotel bar, and/or call it a night. Instead, some well-meaning meeting planner thinks they need an after-dinner speaker. For even greater pitfalls, add a few visiting business associates from foreign countries. Since they don't understand the jokes, they often do as a few Korean executives did once at a program I gave in a little private meeting room in a Nashville hotel. They chatted for a while as I spoke and then stood up and paced back and forth within a few yards of me, looking at their watches.

Often the bad boys in the audience emulate the mischief of rascal kids in school and sit far in the back of the room, where the rest of the audience can't see them but from which vantage point they can torment the speaker and misbehave. Not that long ago, in Elizabethtown, Kentucky, the fellows set up shop at a distant table and made no secret of the fact that they would have preferred talking about basketball and having a few more beers. They kept standing up and waving their dinner napkins at me angrily, shaking their heads disgustedly as I continued to speak, putting their hands over their ears, scratching and stretching, and NOBODY could see them except me.

And don't you know that if I could have figured out a clever way to call attention to them, they would have stopped right away and looked innocent?

You always wonder in a case like that whether to earn the fee by talking the whole fifty minutes or cut it short to put them out of their misery. By now I can figure out ways to cut it short, but no solution is foolproof. IT CAN ALWAYS HAPPEN AGAIN.

18
THE SPEAKER AS LEARNER

Presumably a guest speaker teaches things to the audience. The most highly-paid speakers in the world are the ones who teach How To; they are experts. But I have found that I am the one who learns things from speaking. In an effort to come up with ideas that might be helpful or entertaining to the listeners, I have learned things of immeasurable value to me as a professional person, as a wife and mother and friend.

For one thing, I have realized that one of my mother's favorite old truisms, mentioned to me gently when I was trying to decide which baby-book to follow or which friend's advice to take, was probably the best basic rule of life: This too shall pass. This turned out to be the "message" of many anecdotes.

Daily aggravations, within reason, are not really that bad. The truly terrible things of life are on a far different level. Why get panicked over the small irritations? Of course, I couldn't always keep cool and frequently didn't. I remember those uncool times and regret them in retrospect. But the older I get, the less I sweat the little things. Creating material for my speeches, I found this theory constantly reinforced.

Another thing I learned from giving speeches came to me from a question and answer period after a town hall lecture. I love question and answer periods, probably because I am a ham at heart and have inherited my maternal relatives' inveterate eagerness to continue talking non-stop long after the speech has ended. Even then, I am not as dizzyingly verbal as my mother, who would go into a hardware store for a nail and not emerge until half an hour later, leaving behind a glassy-eyed clerk.

Ask me a question about myself and I'll give a lengthy answer. Privacy is not high enough on my list of personal priorities, I regret to say. Such was the case when someone asked me if I had liked working for Sir Rudolf Bing. I used to reply, "Oh, it was a wonderful and glamorous job! Yes, I loved it," a rather boring and predictable response that I realized one day was inaccurate.

I had loved working at the Metropolitan, I had loved the prestige of working for the general manager, but no, I had not liked working for Sir Rudolf. He was remote and frightening and...and suddenly I understood what it was about him that I had not liked. He never gave a compliment. On the contrary, he watched my moves frowning with nervous apprehension, waiting for the inevitable mistake.

Under these conditions I made dozens of mistakes, some of which I hid brilliantly, others of which he caught and shouted about red-faced. It occurred to me that day during the lecture question-and-answer period that, had Bing told me smilingly on occasion "Good job!," I might even have become a pretty decent secretary. This was clearly the case with his assistant John Gutman, for whom I could even take dictation in foreign languages thanks to his patience, understanding and good humor.

Another thing I have learned from speaking is that honesty generally does turn out to be the best policy. If I use a story that makes me out to be insecure or daffy, then the audience can have the pleasure of laughing with me at my daffiness. When you tell the truth about yourself, preferably when you exaggerate it a little and make it funny, people enjoy it. Perhaps, then, it's wrong for me to call this honesty, because a humorist does exaggerate. But what we exaggerate, generally, is the honest truth.

Honesty, in fact, is something I have come to think about more and more as the years go by. It was only in recent times that I fully understood the famous phrase, "The truth shall set you free." What did that mean? I used to wonder irritably— free from what?

And then one day I understood it, right after an encounter with an elderly friend. I was wearing an attractive but inexpensive strand of metallic beads, one that my daughter Tamara had spotted and bought for me from a sidewalk vendor in New York. My friend, admiring the beads, asked, "Are they fresh-water pearls?"

"Oh gosh, no!" I said. "They're not at all that valuable. Tamara picked them up for me in New York on some street corner."

Impatiently, my friend broke into my explanation. "Never say that!" she snapped vehemently. "They look like fresh-water pearls, and you should call them that. Don't ever down-play yourself."

It struck me at that moment that this dear friend, among many others of my acquaintance, had not only never down-played herself or been apologetic in any way but had, on the contrary, forever UPplayed herself for as long as I had known her. Her form of exaggeration, unlike that of the humorist, was to make herself sound more perfect than she was.

A person can of course do this, exaggerating not only the value of a string of beads but also her family's income, her kids' scores on the SATs and dozens of other things. But when you lie a little, even with the best of intentions, someday you may get caught by the truth—and then you're trapped. You have to remember what your lie was the first time, so that you can repeat it.

If you grin and tell the horrible truth the first time around, you're not trapped at all. You're free. In this respect, one can also go too far. I have a tendency to be absolutely honest about our family's income, a trait that puts me in the distinct minority. I used to enjoy blabbing about how little the university paid my husband, until he nudged me one day and told me to stop talking about it. I had found this form of honesty quite handy in keeping people from asking me to donate money; but my brutal frankness had finally embarrassed the family. So I suppose the best solution is not to talk about it at all. Besides, I have noticed anyway that people only believe you when you lie; go figure.

Just as liberating as telling the truth is the shedding of prejudices. It is not easy to get rid of prejudice, especially when many of the people you know and love have the same prejudices and continue to cling to them.

The first time in my life, for instance, that I attended a social gathering of mixed races and untraditional lifestyles was during my working days in Boston. I heard an opera student make a joke about his own race to a person of another race, just as I do now about my own and my husband's ethnic backgrounds.

As I joined in the general laughter that evening, it struck me with considerable force that this was the first time in my life that I had ever been in a social situation with people of various races and sexual preferences, a gathering where differences were irrelevant and only talent, humor and similar interests counted. And if the differences came up, they were treated with warmth and laughter. Suddenly, I felt almost lightheaded with liberation. I thought, "I have spent a good part of my life worrying about how and when to disapprove of things. I don't NEED to worry, ever, about people's differences or whether my prejudice is justified. It is not only irrelevant, it's foolish. All I need to do is accept people as people."

This was, of course, only the first glimmer of understanding. It took much more time for the lesson to sink in solidly. But the catalyst had been, as it almost always is—humor.

This is not an easy lesson for us to absorb. Since I belong to a very nationalistic minority myself, I know how strongly minorities cling to their own prejudices against other minorities. Perhaps this is why one of my favorite jokes involves two minorities. It's the story I always use as the conclusion to a speech before Greek-Americans.

A Greek arriving in America for the first time upset all his friends by insisting he did not want to go into the restaurant business. "I want to be a cowboy!" he announced.

"NO, Gus!" they all cried. "Greeks eez not cowboys."

He ignored them and set out for the Wild West. In good time he became a first-rate cowboy. One day as he rode the range on his horse, twirling his lasso and watching the tumbleweed drift by, he heard some whooping behind him and turned to see a tribe of Sioux bearing down on him full-speed.

Terrified, the Greek galloped faster and faster, but it was no use. The Indian chief reached him, rode alongside him for a minute, then leaned over and shoved him off his horse. As the Greek hit the ground, the Indian took out his tomahawk.

The poor Greek, realizing his time was near, recalled prayers from his village church. Looking up to heaven, he made the sign of the cross and said, in Greek, "The-eh mou, so-seh meh!" (God, save me!). At this, the Indian dropped his tomahawk and stared at the Greek. "Patrioti!" he cried. "You Greek too?"

One of my most enjoyable speaking markets is that of Greek-American communities. As far as I know, there are very few members of my ethnic group who make a career out of finding humor in it. Only once did I encounter an audience member who seemed offended by humorous ethnic exaggeration, and he was Greek. Perhaps the reason he took offense was that he was probably feeling more American than Greek that night, since he was a member of a serious corporate audience.

After I had told stories that evening about my ethnic childhood to this predominantly Anglo-Saxon group, the man of Greek background approached me with a worried half-smile and asked if he might buy me a cup of coffee and talk a little about our common heritage. His conversation explained the worried look.

"Did your grandmother really have such an accent as you say? Was food really all she cared about? When your father tried so hard to marry you off, was he really this angry-sounding? Was he an uneducated man?"

I confessed that of course I exaggerated their ethnicity a little for the sake of story-telling. He nodded tragically. "Then you must not do this. You have an opportunity as a speaker to show the nobility of your heritage. You can tell people about the great thinkers of the Age of Pericles! Do not make your family out to sound so ordinary. Show the greatness of your heritage!"

"But I'm supposed to be funny," I countered. "Would people laugh if I talked about the nobility of my heritage? Wouldn't they think I was showing off and get embarrassed?"

"It is your duty as a daughter of a great culture!"

I mulled this over but came to the conclusion that, while it might be noble to center my remarks on the greatness of my heritage, it would not be true to what I really am—a humorist. The humorist learns not to take herself so seriously, to look for her own foibles and those of the ones she loves best, and to poke gentle but affectionate fun at them. How else can one be part of the common human experience? We are all in this together, and the more we smile, the more we enjoy it and the better we survive.

Just as I feel it's honest to point out one's faults as well as one's virtues, I feel it is not too honest on the platform—at least for a humorist—to sound too much like an orator. I am not, after all, a debater; I am a down-to-earth storyteller. When people ask for advice on how to speak in public, I tell them with absolute conviction that they must speak exactly as they are talking to me at that moment. The audience, at least for my kind of presentation, should be addressed just as one's dinner guests are addressed at table, with the same good-natured eye contact and smiles and encouraging nods.

This does presuppose that you talk to people at your dinner table in a clear, animated way. Two of the most important pieces of advice I ever got about speaking well came to me long before I had embraced this profession. My mother, who had a very animated voice, had once heard me answering the phone in a monotone in my preteen days. "When you talk on the phone," she told me, "you have to sound lots more alive than when you talk in person. The person on the other end of the phone can't see your face, so you have to put the smile in your voice."

What excellent advice! I have followed it so meticulously over the years that I once frightened a pizza-parlor employee when I called to order the family's supper. "Let me see now," I said excitedly, "I think we'll take a medium. Is that the twelve inch one? No, maybe it better be the large! Hey, kids, do we want mushroom, pepperoni and onions on it?" I chattered on for a minute or two at high and cheerful volume. When I paused for breath, the pizza woman said irritably into the phone, "God, you're hyper!"

Nonetheless I still think Hypervoice on the phone is better than Deadvoice.

The second piece of advice came from Mr. Katz, a drama teacher in college. While directing us in several one-act plays, he told us to find the most important words in the sentence—the focal point of the sentence—and emphasize only those.

Thus, when the flight attendant says in her memorized way, "Please take a moment TO read the instructions ON the safety card IN the seat-back pocket in front of you," my mind boggles. Those aren't the important words.

I'd say that some of the most valuable training for a public speaker, then, might come from a drama course. Actors must learn to communicate with their voices, clearly and naturally.

But how do you remember what you're going to say, they ask? My theory on this is that a speaker, unlike actors, should never memorize, because that can sound stilted from the platform. Worse, you might forget what you memorized. But nobody said you cannot use a crutch. The crutch is not an artificial limb; you don't need to write out every breath and comma, every word you plan to say, which would lead you to sound monotonous.

If, though, it makes you feel comfortable to hold a security blanket, you can write down some clues—which is what I mean by crutch. From these clues, which need be no more than a dozen words or phrases on a card or slip of paper, you can remember a whole story and tell it as you would at the dinner table, with warmth and affection.

Despite my reluctance to insert any sort of motivational message into my speeches, I found after my first few years of humorous speaking that it was difficult to give a "speech" consisting entirely of satirical monologues or anecdotes with-out some theme tying the whole business together.

At first I used my interest in regional accents and types of people as the theme, going from childhood stories to New York memories to impressions of Southerners, to Larry and the kids. I still stick more or less to this format when speaking to a group that requests sheer entertainment, God bless them.

But if they want their people "to come away from the meet-ing with some real message," I have to rethink the anecdotes. And the message is, obviously, about communicating. And relationships. When you're listening instead of talking, you're communicating in the best way. When you watch others instead of thinking only of how you yourself appear, you are paying attention to others. And this is no doubt one of the best possible forms of communicating and of cementing relation-ships.

Best of all, when you put yourself into someone else's place, you are empathizing. This may be the finest form of commu-nication there is and the key to the strongest and best relation-ships.

In looking for family anecdotes with which to illustrate these concepts, I found to my astonishment that some of the things I had tried previously to use for humor were in fact brimming with serious undercurrents.

It had always been part of my accent humor, for example, to point out how careful listening to speech misunderstandings can help you clear up irritating things. It struck me one day that careful listening and watching can also help you uncover marvelous things that had been hidden.

I remembered Mrs. Fischbach. She was a Navy wife who taught Latin at my children's middle school. When my son Nicolai entered eighth grade, I insisted he take Latin, pointing out that it would help with English and give him a strong back-ground in all sorts of other disciplines.

Nicolai, having followed two sisters through school and been compared to them frequently, was not smitten with these disciplines. In most cases the regime of school was not something he looked forward to. But he had discovered that, as a boy with a natural ear for mimicry, he could make his friends laugh. Therefore, to mask any insecurity he might feel in a new classroom, he became the class clown, a circumstance that his classmates loved and the teachers hated.

When Nicolai took Latin, his grade on the first report card was an A. I was stunned and elated and went in for the parent-teacher conference. Mrs. Fischbach greeted me with a large grin and said, "You're Nicolai's mother? He's the funniest kid I have ever met."

"Yes," I whispered, waiting for the reprimand that usually followed this remark.

"When I want the students to read Latin aloud, I get Nicolai up in front of the room. I say, 'Read this like Julius Caesar! Come on, give it all you've got!' And he's hysterical. He acts just like a general, and he reads it as though he's in the movies, with a foreign accent. It sounds exactly the way it should." She paused and chuckled in remembrance. "And his sentences are a scream. Look at this one, when we did the negative interrogative." She showed me on his paper, "Estne Papa Catholicus?" ("Is not the Pope Catholic?")

And then the Navy transferred Mrs. Fischbach's husband to the West Coast and they moved away. A new Latin teacher came in, and Nicolai's second report card grade was D. I went in for the conference.

"You're Nicolai's mother?" said the new teacher, a younger woman with dark hair and heavy eyebrows drawn into a frown. "Well, you have my sympathy. He thinks he's funny. He'll be laughing all the way to the principal's office this year."

Powers of observation, I thought, provide useful information. What she got was a negative impression and she handled it accordingly. Mrs. Fischbach saw the same things but used them in a far different and very marvelous way.

The Latin-class story, then, became a valuable anecdote in message-oriented speaking, as did the experience I had with my second daughter, Tamara, when she was nine years old. Like any child who had begun to appreciate the wonders of gourmet cuisine, she was slightly plump at age nine. Now she's tall and willowy, stopping traffic when she's dressed for a party or strolling on the beach in a new bathing-suit.

But at nine, it was her fate to wear the dreaded Princess Chubbette label on school and party dresses. I couldn't believe it was still around. I had worn it too. It didn't occur to me until recently what a shocking disservice we have done to children in our country by putting huge labels on their clothes marked "Chubbette" or "Husky." Maybe the adults think it's cute and handy. The kids themselves, all of whom can read the labels perfectly well, know it means Fat.

But then we don't always stop to think that children, like adults, are sentient beings, as the rest of this story taught me. We bought Tamara a new Chubbette dress for Easter, and she ran upstairs to my room to try it on the moment we got home from the mall.

Looking at herself in the full-length mirror, she muttered bitterly, "I'm FAT."

I prepared myself at once to give the appropriate Motherlecture. Motherlectures are, of course, filed by category in the brain, some 600 or 700 of them. God forbid you should lose the opportunity to deliver a Motherlecture; you might never get a chance to lecture the child again.

This specific Motherlecture would have gone as follows: "Well, honey, if you think you're a little overweight, we can do something about that. When you come home from school, you come to me for a snack and I'll give you an apple or some carrot sticks instead of cookies, and then we can do a few exercises together, and maybe by Christmas time you'll be nice and slim and you can get a new dress."

But I didn't deliver the lecture. For some unexplainable reason, I uttered the first thing that came into my mind when she stated, "I'm fat." I said, "You think YOU'RE fat!? Look at me!" And I slapped my own hip in a comradely manner. It would have been my automatic response to any adult who had called herself fat.

The opportunity for the Motherlecture was gone forever. But Tamara came across the room to me, small face beaming, and put her arms around me. In a warm, surprisingly adult tone, she said, "I love you, Mama!" And I knew I had done the right thing. I had, in fact, treated her like a stranger instead of my own child—for one would never agree with a stranger who insults herself. To the stranger you offer the courtesy of denial. How rarely do we stop to think that our own flesh and blood might perfectly well deserve this courtesy too?

19
AND IN CONCLUSION . . .

Erma Bombeck once wrote a column I'll remember fondly the rest of my life. The gist was that she figured that she and the President of the United States were the only people in the country who worked at home. She wondered if he ever had to jump up from his desk in the Oval Office to turn off the timer on the ham or shift the load in the washing machine so it would stop buzzing.

You said it, Erma; I can't get a day's work done either for those friendly little interruptions, to say nothing of phone calls from acquaintances who say "Oh, good! I thought you'd be working. Why don't you come to that committee meeting with me this morning. You'd love it!" just when I'm trying to create a mailing that won't be dashed directly into the trash on receipt. Or organize the tax envelopes. Or figure out what new material to tell an audience that is having me back for a second time and is nervous about spending the money.

The problem faced by those of us who get interrupted when we work is that we are at home. If I weren't so afraid of spiders, I would go out and work in the garage and pretend to have an office outside the home.

Until such time as I conquer arachnophobia, I have to try to let Larry run interference. Larry is a formidable answering machine. "Who is this? What do you want? She's busy." If, from up in my little office, I hear his end of this conversation, I generally come barreling down the stairs, frantic to interrupt and say to the intruder, "Oh, he was just kidding! I'm right here, I'm not doing a THING!"

But his methods are excellent when dealing with unwanted phone solicitations. The moment I hear the dreaded scripted words, "Is this the lady of the house? How are you this evening, ma'am?" I tell the caller to hold on and I rush to tell

Larry to pick up the phone. I can't forget how brilliantly he handled the light bulb lady. The first time she called, selling light bulbs that never blow out and cost only $9.95 each, I felt sorry for her because she sounded so miserable and I ordered one. It blew out, and I could only get my money back if I returned the bulb, carefully packaged in its original carton, to Hong Kong.

Therefore the second time the light bulb lady called—as always at about nine o'clock on a Sunday morning—I hurried upstairs and woke late-sleeping Larry, telling him "Honey, please talk to the light bulb lady. I feel sorry for her but I don't want to hurt her feelings! Could you turn her down as nicely as possible?"

He picked up the phone and yelled, in a tone that carried to Hong Kong, "WE DON WAN' LIGHT BOLBS! DON'T CALL AGAIN!" and hung up.

If a recording calls me and asks me to wait for the tone so I can leave my name and address to receive detailed information about some wonderful time-share property, I listen respectfully to the entire lengthy come-on full of Madison Avenue exaggerations and then, when the beep sounds, I say, "I dun spik English."

Of course it's not just the telephone that prevents me from doing all the fiendishly important paperwork that any self-employed person should be doing to further her career. There are other things of vital concern, such as going out again to look at the tomato plants, to see if perhaps the green, golf-ball-sized tomato I looked at this morning has by afternoon become large and red enough to be picked.

Or I could go weigh myself again. Because I have been tainted by the current maniacal self-image climate of the United States, in which models and beauty queens 5'11" tall tell us they weigh 105 pounds and wear size two dresses even though they look perfectly normal in their pictures, I too have developed an obsessive relationship with the bathroom scales. Ignoring the sage advice of diet gurus to avoid weighing yourself more than once a week, I head first thing to the scales in the morning.

After the initial shock of seeing that I gained a pound overnight, I take a shower and weigh myself again. Aha, I seem to have lost half a pound! Could it have been dirt? I comb my hair and check the old scales again, stepping on them very carefully so that no one in the house will hear them whirring and catch me at my fanaticism. Good grief, I've gained two pounds. It must be those damned hairpins.

"All right, Hope," I whisper to myself furiously, "control yourself and do not step on these scales again until bedtime." But I'm smart enough to avoid them at bedtime because I know I weigh more than ever at night.

By the time I have avoided my office successfully by checking the tomato and the scales and answering a few phone calls from relatives or from organizations that want me to come speak for nothing, it's time to cook something. If I'm crafty, I can avoid work altogether by remembering that the curtains in the back room have not been washed for fifteen years. I even go so far as to wash a pair sometimes, though they disintegrate in the washing machine—my mother would have put them in the bathtub, of course, but that's a lot like work—and now I have to figure out where one goes to buy curtains.

In an effort to ensure that I'm always too busy to do work in my office, I have taken up several other delightful jobs in my hometown. Alas, the kinds of jobs that appeal to me pay virtually nothing. But what more pleasant way could there be to earn money, even at a low part-time level, than to use one's voice for radio commercials. From time to time a local recording studio calls me in to do a character voice. Like the other talent, I come at the appointed time and am handed a script I have never seen before. We go into the studio, where the offhand banter and sarcasm are at a level of wit that network television would be desperate to achieve, and with barely a glance at the script beforehand we plunge into a reading of a commercial just faxed in by an advertising agency in some distant city.

In just a few takes we're finished and off we go, back to our normal jobs. This is the joy of radio. It doesn't matter what anything looks like; all the creativity must come from the voice. I have done two television commercials in my time, and each was a nightmare of pretentious tedium that required seven or eight hours of rehearsal and filming and refilming to produce a spot that lasted at most one minute.

One particularly memorable radio spot which I performed with a witty, gravel-voiced friend had us cast as two chickens in a Tennessee egg factory. We were to have a normal conversation, sounding as much like chickens as we could manage, and I had to lay an egg towards the end of the script. It didn't take much rehearsal for us to achieve hen-sounding cackling voices and, for the egg, I just did my favorite old barnyard chicken imitation, the one I've been doing since grammar school, and the sound effect guys made a popping sound that clearly indicated the production of the egg.

I also do a good cat fight but there hasn't been much call for it. To keep in practice, I go out on the back porch and perform it sometimes when there are real cats fighting and/or mating out in the neighbor's back yard. My son Nicolai, however, is the champion in animal sounds. His moo is so authentic he has started riots at dairies. How desperately I envy his talent!

Another good way to keep visible—or, let's face it, invisible—in my hometown is to perform on public radio. In a moment of ill-advised good nature, the program manager of the local fine-arts station hired me to do a weekly program on opera. This gives me a chance for appalling irreverence and highly subjective musical choices. It might not make me as famous as I could be if I were a rock-and-roll disk jockey, but there is great pleasure in having someone whirl around in a store when I speak to a salesperson and cry, "You're Hope! I recognize your voice."

In addition to these extra income-producing activities, I take on a gigantic assignment that doesn't pay at all but is a totally logical volunteer job for me—board member of the Virginia

Opera. Naturally, with my previous operatic affiliations, I was a logical choice for enlistment in the formation of this regional company in 1974.

A first-rate company, the Virginia Opera uses my services just as you might imagine, for public relations events, wild and irreverent spoofs at fund-raisers and even for actual productions. They have been very nice about letting me disrupt serious shows with my peculiar behavior as an extra or in a cameo non-singing role. When I performed Ida in *Die Fledermaus*, the scenic designer thought I looked so much like a television series star named Flo in my make-up and wig, he persuaded me to interpolate Flo's famous line, "Kiss my grits!" into a scene in the second act. The critic, whose sense of humor was not on our wave length, had apoplexy.

Causing trouble as Ida (Hope, R.) in **Die Fledermaus** *at the Virginia Opera, 1983.*

If local radio listeners don't always recognize my voice, they might instead spot my hair. I have been wearing my hair in the same, pseudo-classical puffy French twist for—at this writing—THIRTY YEARS. Once I saw a program on Oprah Winfrey in which three women were hauled in front of the cameras and interviewed, accompanied by roars of laughter and shouts of disbelief from the audience, because they hadn't changed their hairstyles for ten years.

Some people don't mind my sameness of hairdo at all and, noting that by now it has become an odd trademark, beseech me urgently never to change it. Others—and this includes my college roommate who only sees me every six to ten years and feels the same stab of concern each time at the sight of my eternal head—are desperate to get me to do something that's more in style. They utter the dreaded tactful phrase,"You know, I'd like to see you try something a little different. . .", a phrase I know well is a euphemism for "You look WEIRD."

My own feeling is that my hairstyle is not that weird unless I'm wearing slacks, in which case, granted, I look incongruous. You really shouldn't have an ancient Greek head on top of an Annie Oakley body. Some of us were meant, unfortunately, to wear togas, but they went out of style.

Now that I am easing into the category of Wiser Old Generation, I begin at last to follow the courage of my convictions when shopping and not tremble lest my choice bring derision or unsolicited advice down on my head. This fear of advice surely comes from shopping expeditions with my Aunt Connie, the beloved relative of Bridal Set renown.

Being a woman who cared what others thought, wore, and did more than anyone I'll ever know, Aunt Connie despaired of my lack of interest in the Things Girls Are Supposed to Care About. From time to time she would call my mother and announce that she wanted to take me shopping "for something nice for the Christmas season." Bless her heart, she clung mistakenly to the hope that somebody might ask me to a dance, the way beaus used to do in the '20s.

I realize now that I approached these trips with far more horror and trepidation than gratitude because I knew that her motive was long-suffering. Perhaps subconsciously she, too, knew that her generosity did not spring from unconditional affection; she just thought I looked dowdy and hoped to cure it.

If I reached for something odd that I thought might look a little like Me, Aunt Connie would inevitably frown and murmur, "They're not wearing that, dear," and the platoon of hov-

Hope and Larry dressed up for the Virginia Opera Ball, 1989.

ering saleswomen, all of them long-time cronies whom she called occasionally by their last names ("Byrd, ask McMillan if she put aside that little brown outfit") would nod cryptically in agreement and say, "You just listen to your awnt, dawlin'; she knows clothes."

For years, even without Aunt Connie around, I bought things that saleswomen or shopping-trip companions told me I ought to have even when my gut told me No. But now that I'm older than the saleswomen and know how much the monthly mortgages cost, it's harder to put one over on me. Well, almost.

Another astonishing aspect of middle-age is getting used to the fact that our children are adults. My husband and I have fought this all the way. It is a wonder they have the independent spirits they have, with us practically chewing their meals for them in traditional old-country fashion.

For example, our two daughters teach English in foreign countries and sometimes we don't see them for year-long periods. Yet their letters are wonderful and their experiences incomparable, so we would not dream of trying to dissuade them.

Penny, though a Russian major at Princeton, went to China to teach right after graduation. It soon became clear that her quick wit, enthusiasm and love of languages made her ideally suited to the profession. At this writing, she has just been evacuated—under gunfire—from Yemen and her journals read like a wild adventure story. But Penny seems to attract disaster wherever she travels.

The whole family descending on Penny's college graduation—left to right: Nicolai, Vaga, Penny, Hope, Tamara, Larry.

Chernobyl blew up when she went to Russia and she was in China during the Beijing student revolution. To our tentative relief, however, she lived in Dalian, where her students were enthusiastic young engineers at the Institute of Technology. Penny began to learn Chinese rapidly and told us with pleasure that we could direct-dial her dormitory in Dalian with no problem, provided we remembered what time it was over there. We soon realized that it would have been wise for us to learn a little Chinese as well.

The first time I direct-dialed, the dorm switchboard operator answered, "Hu-eh!" Brilliantly, I gleaned that this might be Hello, so I responded, "Hu-eh!" and then, in laborious English, began, "May I please speak..." at which the operator promptly hung up.

"Larry!" I yelled. "We just lost about ten dollars!"

"Try it again," he said. "At least we know we can reach China." This counted for a lot, because when Penny had spent a semester in Moscow, no amount of advance reservation with AT&T or anybody else could ensure us a phone call to the USSR. "Ve haff finished our quota of phone calls for today," one Soviet operator announced, to which Larry responded volubly with Russian curses.

So I direct-dialed Dalian again and we went through the "Hu-eh!" routine. This time I shouted, slowly, "PEN-NY MI-HA.." and she hung up a second time.

"Twenty bucks gone!" I called to Larry.

"Try one more time."

This time even I could detect a note of impatience in the "Hu-eh." I said, "AMERICAN TEACHER.." and, miraculously, there was a buzz and Penny came on the line. "Listen," I cried, "before you do another thing, teach me to ask for you in Chinese."

"Try asking for my room number," she advised. "Say 'Jo-wuh-SUHH' and be sure you pronounce it exactly like that, or else you might be saying something entirely different and maybe even obscene."

My Chinese vocabulary is now limited to "Hu-eh" and "Jo-wuh-suhh" but Penny can carry on a marvelous conversation with servers and owners in any Chinese restaurant in the United States. After all, she had to speak the language in order to avoid being served stir-fried porcupine and fox terrier when in restaurants in China. And why not, we finally conceded, in contemplating their cuisine; they seemed equally appalled at the Americans' fondness for cheese and hamburger.

Tamara, an art history major at Vassar, has also found English teaching abroad a marvelous way to see the world. Her wise and affectionate nature, lively humor and sensitivity have been balms to us all since she was tiny and have served her well as a teacher in Europe and Thailand. But her real love is art, her own and other people's. Her paintings do us proud, brightening the walls of our house, cottage, galleries and businesses. Her writing, too, is a joy, economical and evocative, and the arrival of a letter from her with a foreign postmark is an occasion for much rejoicing.

As for Nicolai the expert cow-imitator, there came a time when he asked us worriedly what he should major in at the University of North Carolina in Asheville—worriedly because the standard curriculum and usual measures loomed before him unappealingly like an Everest he must scale exactly as everyone else did. Remembering the dozens of times we had all rolled on the floor weak with laughter at his imitations of people and incidents, I said, "Why don't you take drama?"

Aghast, he replied, "Ma! What would I do with drama?"

"That's a parent's question," I said, knowing what a feeling he would get from doing for academic credit something he liked to do and did well.

Now, like all other theater majors, he goes to television and theater auditions, appears in commercials and holds a variety of jobs. We're satisfied, but strangers aren't, especially foreigners. "I am amazed," said an Eastern European woman whom I had just met, "that you allow your son to do such a foolish thing. How will he make financial success?"

But how could she know that, in terms of success, the two awards achieved by Nicolai in his school days are among my greatest treasures—a medal for being "Kindest Boy in Mrs. Lingo's Third Grade" and his election as Class Clown in his senior year in high school.

Besides, maybe some day he'll get us free tickets to his shows.

What I have learned from inviting audiences and readers into my private life is something more valuable than I had anticipated—the knowledge of how best to handle the rest of my life.

In remembering things about my parents and grandparents, friends and employers, husband and children, so that I might share them in some enlightening way with my listeners, I have learned lessons. Some decisions were the right ones, others were wrong. Some memories should be savored, others forgotten. This was worth being angry about; that was bad at the time but funny in retrospect. And . . . this too shall pass.

The lessons are not always easy, and I still forget about them. Or ignore them. When you juggle around a lot of likes, dislikes, duties, pleasures, obligations, loved ones or nuisances, you often lose your balance. Who ever said it would be easy?

Whether or not you're a humorist, you can entertain the people around you. Whether or not you know them well, you can make them feel like friends.

And even if you're no more Greek than sushi, you can come bearing gifts. The nicest gift is a part of yourself—the gift of a smile that lingers, like that of the Cheshire cat, long afterwards.

ABOUT THE AUTHOR

Hope Mihalap, an award-winning humorist, was born in Virginia, graduated from Vassar College, and worked as private secretary to two of the most renowned leaders in the world of opera—Boris Goldovsky and Sir Rudolf Bing.

She went on to become a newspaper columnist and radio personality. Now she is a humorous public speaker sought after for convention keynotes, town halls and spouse programs. She has been awarded the Mark Twain Award for Humor by the International Platform Association and the Council of Peers Award of Excellence by the National Speakers Association. She lives in Norfolk, VA, with her husband, a professor emeritus of Russian. They have three children who work all over the world. For relaxation, Hope likes to cook and read mysteries.

Hope's presentations are tailored to each audience and include favorite stories about herself and her family, observations on good communicating, witty words on cultural diversity and an occasional wacky look at the world of performing arts.

To inquire about booking Hope for your next program write:

Hope Mihalap
711 Stockley Gardens, #2
Norfolk, VA 23507

Phone: 757-623-0429   **Fax: 757-489-0007**

FOR YOUR NEXT PROGRAM. . .

Consider one of Hope's witty, tailor-made presentations:

Where There's Hope, There's Laughter—A hilarious trip with Hope through some of her life's experiences, full of accent humor, wry observations and good will.

Bean by Bean: A Sackful of Experience—The Greeks have a saying: Bean by bean, the sack gets full. Every small "bean" or happening is an important part of the full sack of life. Hope shows how some remembered beans, or kernels, of experience have enriched her own life and reminds you how to keep count of your own.

Play It By Ear: The Best Way to Communicate—Good communication and solid relationships—at home or in the workplace—boil down to the Three E's: Ears, Eyes and Empathy. Learn how the Three E's can help you get along happily with others.

From Opera to Uproar—Opera isn't always such serious business. Hope's experiences in the world of this temperamental and fascinating art form can keep you laughing and teach you a lot about one of the greatest shows on earth.

Swimming Through the Melting Pot—A witty and educational presentation on the humor and charms of global diversity.

These programs, and others customized to your group, are available in varying lengths both as keynotes and half-day presentations. For information on booking Hope Mihalap as a speaker, use the information below:

Hope Mihalap
711 Stockley Gardens, #2
Norfolk, VA 23507

Phone: 757-623-0429   **Fax: 757-489-0007**

TO ORDER

MAIL ORDER TO: **H M BOOKS**
711 Stockley Gardens #2
Norfolk, VA 23507

	AMOUNT	FOR
Please send _____ copies of the book, **WHERE THERE'S HOPE** $12.50 EACH	$	books
Please send _____ copies of the cassette, **WHERE THERE'S HOPE, THERE'S LAUGHTER:** 45-minute live performance. Audio cassette $10.00 EACH	$	cassette
Please send _____ copies of the cassette, **IT'S GREEK TO US!:** 45-minute live bilingual performance, for audiences of Greek background. Audio cassette $10.00 EACH	$	cassette
Add for shipping/handling 1 to 3 copies, books or cassettes $2.50. Add .50 @ additional book or cassette.	$	postage
VIRGINIA RESIDENTS ADD 4½% SALES TAX	$	tax
Enclosed is ❑ check for or ❑ money order. **U S Funds Only.**	$	**TOTAL**

Make check payable to: H M Books

U S Funds only, please

Name: _____

Address: _____

City, State _____ Zip _____

Phone: _____

PLEASE ALLOW 4-6 WEEKS DELIVERY TIME.